Fall 2013–2015

Achim Menges

# Material Performance: Fibrous Tectonics & Architectural Morphology

Harvard University
Graduate School of Design

## Material Performance: Fibrous Tectonics & Architectural Morphology

This studio explores material performance, its manifold and deep interrelations with technology, biology, and culture. It focuses on fiber-composite materials as vehicles for inquiry, since fibrous systems are omnipresent in natural structures, form part of the most advanced material technologies, and are at the same time deeply rooted in the history and culture of material practices. However, in architecture, technical fiber-composite materials, such as glass- or carbon-fiber reinforced plastics, are usually considered to be "amorphic," meaning they fully depend on a mold or formwork to obtain a specific shape and structure. This studio challenges this common conception in a multifaceted manner. Instead of understanding fibrous form as being obedient to a mold, this studio strives to reveal the "morphic" character of fibrous systems and discover their inherent tectonic qualities and spatial characteristics.

**Studio Instructor**
Achim Menges

**Students**
**2013** Georgios Athanasopoulos, Joon Hyuk Choe, Brian Chu, Kevin Hinz, Alexander Jacobson, Jeonghyun Kim, Zunheng Lai, Tristan McGuire, Sunchung Min, Rachel Moranis, Catherine Soderberg, Thena Tak, Arthur Terry, Jun Wang

**2014** Alice Chai, Erin Cuevas, Niccolo Dambrosio, Iman Fayyad, Joshua Feldman, Michael Johnson, Wenling Li, Ping Lu, Jana Masset, Christopher Meyer, Nancy Nichols, Chase Pitner, Stefan Stanojevic

**2015** Yuan Gao, Feijiao Huo, Xin Ji, Demir Purisic, Marysol Rivas Brito, Gavin Ruedisueli, Zahra Safaverdi, Man Su, Joseph Varholick, Junko Yamamoto

**Workshop Experts**
Moritz Dörstelmann, Marshall Prado

**Teaching Assistance**
Puja Patel, Alexander Jacobson, Christopher Meyer

2015 Final Studio Review featuring guest critics: Axel Kilian, Brandon Clifford, Mariana Ibañez, Panagiotis Michalatos, and Jenny Sabin

Studio Agenda


10 **Material Performance: Fibrous Tectonics and Architectural Morphology**
Achim Menges

18 **Integrative Design and Fabrication Methodologies for Fibrous Systems**
Marshall Prado, Moritz Dörstelmann


Studio Projects


26 **Armature Surface**
Kevin Hinz, Alexander Jacobson, Thena Tak

42 **Fiber Space Reciprocities**
Georgios Athanasopoulos, Brian Chu

58 **Pneumatic Fibrous Form**
Erin Cuevas, Mike Johnson, Jana Masset

76 **Form-Active Fibrous-Composite Structural Surface**
Wenling Li, Christopher Meyer, Chase Pitner

94 **Studies in Fiber Interaction**
Iman Fayyad, Joshua Feldman

112 **An Architectonic Notion for Knitting and Pneumatics**
Yuan Gao, Demir Purisic, Zahra Safaverdi, Joseph Varholick


Critics' Responses


136 **What is the Question?**
Johan Bettum

138 **Fibrous Structures Studio**
Axel Kilian

140 **Biosynthetic Digital Handcraft**
Jenny Sabin

144 Contributors

2014 Research Project *Slack Systems* by Alice Chai, Nancy Nichols

Studio
Agenda

01

# Material Performance: Fibrous Tectonics and Architectural Morphology

Achim Menges

*In one philosophy one thinks of form or design as primarily conceptual or cerebral, something to be generated as a pure thought in isolation from the messy world of matter and energy. Once conceived, a design can be given a physical form by simply imposing it on a material substratum, which is taken to be homogeneous, obedient and receptive to the wishes of the designer. The opposite stance may be represented by a philosophy of design in which materials are not inert receptacles for a cerebral form imposed from the outside, but active participants in the genesis of form. This implies the existence of heterogeneous materials, with variable properties and idiosyncrasies which the designer must respect and make an integral part of the design which, it follows, cannot be routinized.*
—Manuel De Landa

A new understanding of the material in architecture is beginning to arise. No longer are we bound to conceive the digital realm as separated from the physical world. Instead we can explore computation as an intense interface to material and vice versa. Thus materiality no longer remains a fixed property and passive receptor of form, but it transforms into an active generator of design. Accordingly, and in contrast to linear and mechanistic modes of fabrication and construction, materialization now begins to coexist with design as explorative robotic processes.[1] This presents a radical departure from both the trite modernist "truth to materials" and the dismissal of material altogether as emblematic for the previous generation of digital architecture.

The studio embraces this particular contemporary condition of architecture, and thus seeks to investigate the notion of material performance as a vehicle for design exploration and critical inquiry. By nature, this requires focusing on a specific material, as only an in-depth study and intense engagement with the materiality and the related processes of materialization enables innovation that challenges entrenched design thinking and established constructional logics. Due to its manifold and deep interrelations with technology, biology, and culture, a material domain that appears to be especially suited for this investigation are fibrous composites, such as glass- or carbon-fiber reinforced plastics, which have become the focal point of this design research studio over the past three years.

Fiber-Reinforced Plastics (FRP) joined the palette of building materials fairly late. Processes for mass-producing FRP were first developed in the early 1930s under the brand name Fiberglass, and, once suitable resins were introduced, taken up by the shipbuilding and aircraft industries. After the war, designers began experimentation with these novel material systems, with Charles and Ray Eames being among the first. In architecture, FRP experienced a first peak in the 1950s and 1960s mainly with experimental house designs,

such as the Monsanto House of the Future and Matti Suuronen's Futuro Houses. Both employ glass-fiber composites to break formal and spatial norms of the time. However, these projects can still be considered as belonging to an initial phase of borrowing design concepts and mimicking constructional logics of preceding materials, as is most often the case when new materials are introduced in architecture. With the oil crisis of 1973, petroleum-heavy plastics was unattractive to most architects, before the inherent materiality of these fibrous systems was fully explored.

The introduction of both computer-aided design (CAD) and computer-aided manufacturing (CAM) in architectural practice in the 1990s led to a renewed interest in FRP. These digital technologies triggered a desire for freeform surface while also providing suitable production processes. But the underlying conception

2013 Research Project *Morphogenetic Fibrous Gradience* by Zunheng Lai, Jun Wang.

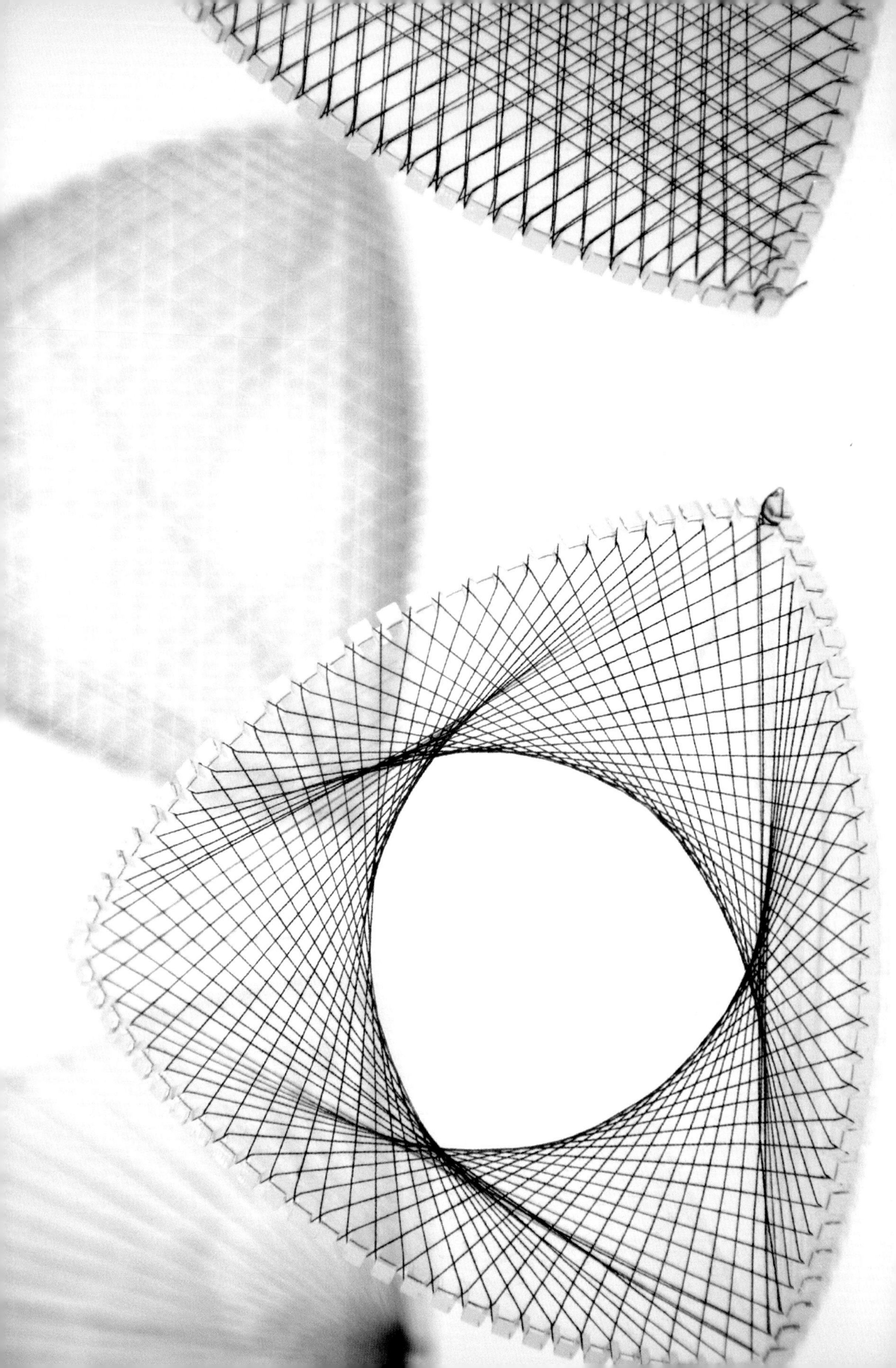

of the materials remained unchallenged, as fiber-composites were, and usually still are, considered to be amorphic—that is, intrinsically formless and thus dependent on external formwork. This still applies to most uses of fiber-composites in the building sector, as well as the automotive, naval, and aerospace industries, where composites have found a much wider application. What they still all share, though, is the dependency on material-shaping devices, in other words some kind of mold. These molding techniques range from fiber placement and fiber layup applications on external, positive, and negative molds to fiber pultrusion dies, to filament winding on internal male mandrels.

The studio seeks to challenge this conception. Instead of understanding fibrous form as being obedient to a predefined mold, it strives to reveal the "morphic" character of fibrous systems and discover their inherent material gestalt and architectural potential. In this way, the studio seeks to investigate fibrous composite in a twofold manner: First, there is the pragmatic need to overcome the necessity for comprehensive molds, as their expense (for serial production) or wastefulness (for one-offs) reduces the architectural application of FRP to repetitious components or big-budget projects. Second, and more importantly, there is the design interest in engaging the self-expression of the material as a designer driver. Employing advanced computational design, simulation, and fabrication allows addressing both points by creatively engaging the specific material performance and filamentous character of fibrous composite systems, which is at the same time technically innovative and intellectually elegant.

**Studio Context: Biology and Enabling Technologies**

To reposition fibrous systems in architecture, the study of natural fiber structures appears as important as the investigation of technical precedents. Natural and man-made fiber-composites are comparable, as they share their fundamental structural logic, with both systems composed of fibrous elements embedded in a matrix material. From those two compositional elements almost all load-bearing biological structures are built, and, even more surprisingly given the diverse spectrum of systems and traits, nature uses only four basic fibrous materials for this: cellulose, collagen, chitin, and silk.[2] The astounding level of diversity, performance capacity, and material resourcefulness observed in living nature unfolds from the differentiation of fiber organization, density and arrangement across multiple levels of hierarchy.[3]

A second critical component for rethinking fibrous composites is the development of new modes of production. As a point of departure for the studio's architectural speculation, serve the technological developments of the ICD Institute for Computational Design (Professor Achim Menges) and the ITKE Institute for Building Structures and Structural Design (Professor Jan Knippers) at the University of Stuttgart. Over the past few years their collaborative research has explored the transfer of morphological principles of fibrous structures from nature to architecture, with a particular focus on the related development of robotic, moldless, or coreless fabrication processes.

The first phase of this research investigated a continuous, single-layer shell and innovative coreless winding processes through understanding the differentiated fiber structure of the exoskeleton of arthropods resulting in the ICD/ITKE Research Pavilion 2012.[4] In this process, a full surface mandrel was reduced to a simple linear scaffolding allowing the first layer of glass-fiber to serve as the embedded mold for the structural carbon-fiber layers.[5] In the second phase, the research culminating in the subsequent ICD/ITKE Research Pavilion 2013–14 was based on morphological principles of the hardened, yet very lightweight, double-layered fibrous shell that constitutes the forewings of flying beetles.[6] This second phase further reduced the need for a mold by developing a novel coreless fiber-winding process to fabricate highly differentiated composite elements between two collaborating robots using an adjustable toolkit.[7] In phase three, the research scope expanded from morphological principles to procedural logics of fiber layup processes in biology, specifically the subaquatic webs of water spiders. Water spiders create livable habitats by trapping an air bubble then structurally reinforcing the interior with silk fibers. Following extensive research on this process, the ICD/ITKE Research Pavilion 2014–15 was fabricated by developing a robotic process of applying fibers along the inside of a inflatable membrane.[8] Once sufficient fibers were laid to form a self-supporting structure, the initial pressure allowing the pneumatic surface to serve as a mold was released and then employed as a building skin.

The research by ICD/ITKE enables us to understand fibrous composites no longer as

Previous page: 2015 Research Project *Soft Control Fiber System* by Feijiao Huo, Xin Ji, Man Su Junko Yamamoto.

merely passive receptacles of form imposed by a fixed and static mold, but rather as the critical constituents in a design methodology that employs the very materiality and related materialization processes as generative drivers.[9] The studio seeks to explore the spatial ramifications and architectural consequences of such novel enabling technologies in order to investigate the related notion of fibrous tectonics and, through this, to foster material-oriented design thinking.

**Studio Structure: Toward Fibrous Morphology in Architecture**

The studio aims to introduce students to a design approach that bridges the cultural and technical dimension of fibrous materials in architecture and the rich repertoire of fibrous material organization in nature. Therefore, students investigate fiber-composite materials, experiment hands-on with related robotic fiber lay-up and filament-winding processes, and pursue the development of fibrous systems in architecture as novel spatial and structural possibilities. Throughout this inquiring, the studio foregrounds design research during the entire term, which is structured in the following phases.

**Phase 1: Knowledge-Building**

Each semester students undertake collaborative research into specific topics relevant tothe entire studio development in order to produce a shared pool of resources and expertise.

Topics explored include (1) Fibrous Systems in Biology, (2) Fibrous Materials in Technology, (3) Fibrous Fabrication in Technology with a focus on advanced fabrication processes for fiber-reinforced composites, (4) Fibrous Systems in Architecture from historical to cutting-edge projects and experiments, and (5) Fibrous Systems in Experimental Design Research foregrounding innovation in speculative projects and design. The results of this research are accumulated in a foundational research document used by all students for technological, biological, and cultural reference.

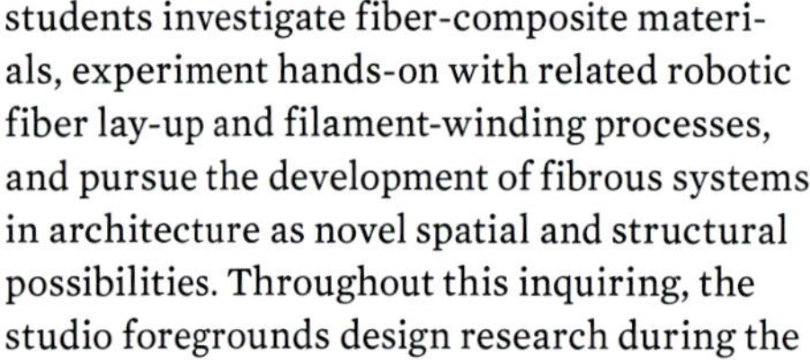

Top, left: ICD/ITKE Research Pavilion 2012. Right: Related robotic fabrication process. Bottom, left: ICD/ITKE Research Pavilion 2013–14. Right: related filament-winding process.

Following page: 2014 Research Project *Nature of bi-stability in composite structures* by Niccolo Dambrosio, Ping Lu, Stefan Stanojevic.

**Phase 2: Concurrent Design Syntax and Material System Development**

Following the research phase, students focus on establishing design matrices of fibrous structures, indicating their variable tectonic potentials. The aim is to develop a design syntax that incorporates the logics of the fiber-distribution process. Initially expressed as pseudo-code in plain English and executed through manual fiber lay-up, these algorithmic processes enable the investigation of the relation between the underlying scaffold, the process sequences, and the resulting fibrous structures. The variables of both the scaffold and the process are explored in a comparative manner, altering one parameter at a time and resulting in graphical and physical matrices that indicate the interrelation between scaffold parameters, process parameters, and resulting material system. The developed matrices graphically represent the algorithmic logic and physically demonstrate the resultant fibrous structures.

**Phase 3: Spatial Fibrous Morphology**

These matrices are then synthesized into an initial, larger-scale fibrous morphology demonstrating spatial hierarchy. In addition to the local and regional fibrous logics this phase requires the inclusion of a global geometry. The prototype is conceived as a first test of spatial and structural potentials of fibrous systems. As a result, students develop a comprehensive definition of the prototype morphology, followed by the fabrication of a spatial fibrous morphology prototype through robotic fiber lay-up or filament-winding technique.

**Phase 4: Spatial, Structural and Tectonic Potentials of Fibrous Morphology Prototype**

Development of the fibrous morphology prototypes is continued through spatial, structural, and tectonic potentials in relation to morphological features and the underlying drivers of the fiber-distribution process. System characteristics and features are defined in regards to surface openings, surface opacity/translucency/transparency, inhabitable surfaces, surface structure, system/ground relation, mold/scaffold integration, hard/soft transition, or continuity and modularity.

**Phase 5: Proto-architectural Fibrous Morphology**

The final phase of the studio explores a possible synthesis of the previous phases through the digital development and physical construction of a scale model of the proto-architectural, fibrous morphology. This provides the opportunity to enable and address different spatial morphologies, multiple-performance criteria, and abstracted-site topography. The final scale model is accompanied by a partial full-scale demonstrator indicating the system-buildup and surface qualities.

The main objective of the studio is to expose students to a design approach that conceives of materiality and materialization as an active generator of form, space, and structure, which enables the uncovering of novel tectonics and formerly unexplored architectural morphologies. The intense engagement with the material, together with the rigorous yet open-ended exploration of its performances, aims at triggering a curiosity and criticality that challenges disciplinary conventions of entrenched design methodology and established tectonic systems. In this way, the studio seeks not only to build material understanding and related design sensitivity among the students. It also aims to trace the emergence of new material cultures in architecture within the context of the ever-accelerating integrative technologies of design computation and robotic fabrication, which will have a profound impact on the material practice of the next generation of architects.

1 A. Menges (ed.), "Material Synthesis–Fusing the Physical and the Computational," *Architectural Design*, Vol. 85, No. 5, (2015).

2 George Jeronimidis, "Structure-Property Relationships in Biological Materials / Design and Function of Structural Biological Materials," in M. Elices (ed), *Structural Biological Materials*, 2000: 3–30.

3 George Jeronimidis, "Biodynamics," in M. Hensel, A. Menges, and M. Weinstock (eds), "Emergence: Morphogenetic Design Strategies," *Architectural Design*, Vol 74, No 3, (2004): 90–9.

4 ICD/ITKE Research Pavilion 2012, Stuttgart: Researchers and students of ICD Institute for Computational Design (Prof. Achim Menges) and ITKE Institute of Building Structures and Structural Design (Prof. Jan Knippers), University of Stuttgart in collaboration with Institute of Evolution and Ecology, Department of Evolutionary Biology of Invertebrates (Prof. Oliver Betz) and Centre for Applied Geoscience, Department of Invertebrates-Paleontology, University of Tübingen (Prof. James Nebelsick), ITV Denkendorf (Dr. Markus Milwich).

5 Steffen Reichert, Tobias Schwinn, Markus Gabler, Riccardo La Magna, Frédéric Waimer, Jan Knippers, Achim Menges, "Fibrous Structures: An Integrative

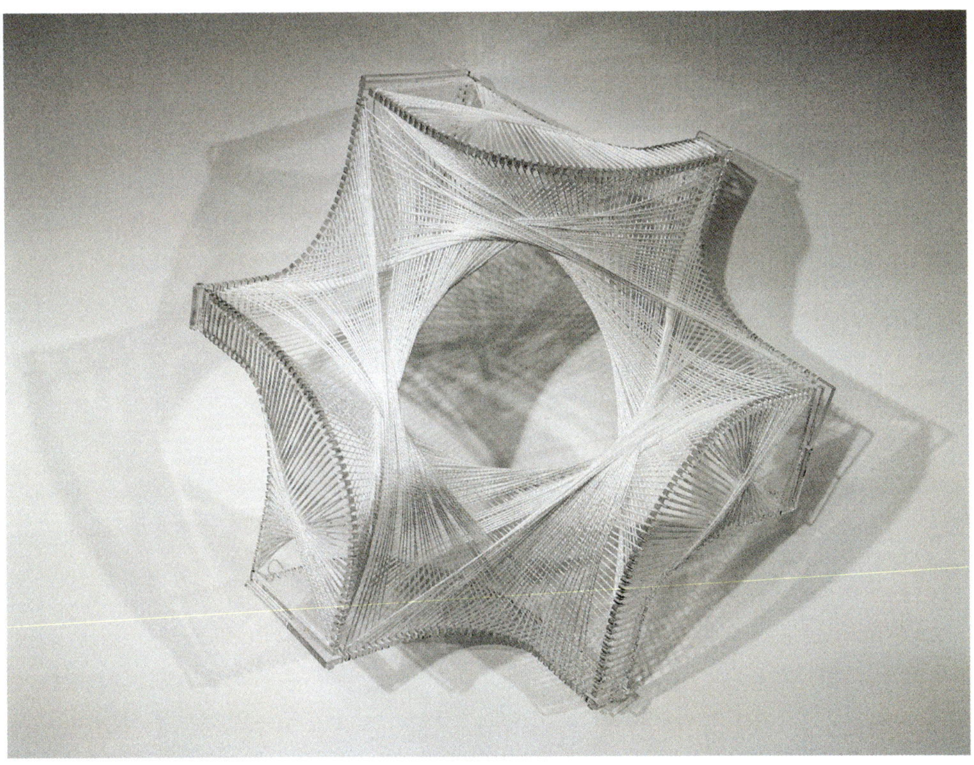



Approach to Design Computation, Simulation and Fabrication for Lightweight, Glass and Carbon-Fiber-Composite Structures in Architecture Based on Biomimetic Design Principles," *CAD Journal*, Volume 52, (July 2014): 27–39.

6 ICD/ITKE Research Pavilion 2013–14, Stuttgart: Researchers and students of ICD Institute for Computational Design (Prof. Achim Menges) and ITKE Institute of Building Structures and Structural Design (Prof. Jan Knippers), University of Stuttgart; in collaboration with Institute of Evolution and Ecology, Department of Evolutionary Biology of Invertebrates (Prof. Oliver Betz) and Centre for Applied Geoscience, Department of Invertebrates-Paleontology, University of Tübingen (Prof. James Nebelsick), ANKA / Institute for Photon Science and Synchrotron Radiation (Prof. Tilo Baumbach), Karlsruhe Institute of Technology; ITV Denkendorf (Dr. Markus Milwich).

7 Moritz Dörstelmann, Stefana Parascho, Marshall Prado, Achim Menges, Jan Knippers, Integrative Computational Design Methodologies for Modular Architectural Fiber-composite Morphologies, in Design Agency [Proceedings of the 34th Annual Conference of the Association for Computer Aided Design in Architecture (ACADIA)], Los Angeles, (2014): 219–228.

8 ICD/ITKE Research Pavilion 2014–15, Stuttgart: Researchers and students of ICD Institute for Computational Design (Prof. Achim Menges) and ITKE Institute of Building Structures and Structural Design (Prof. Jan Knippers), University of Stuttgart; in collaboration with Institute of Evolution and Ecology, Department of Evolutionary Biology of Invertebrates (Prof. Oliver Betz) and Centre for Applied Geoscience, Department of Invertebrates-Paleontology, University of Tübingen (Prof. James Nebelsick).

9 A. Menges and J. Knippers, "Fibrous Tectonics," *Architectural Design*, Vol. 85, No. 5, (2015): 40–47.

2013 Research Project *Morphogenetic Fibrous Gradience* by Zunheng Lai, Jun Wang.

# Integrative Design and Fabrication Methodologies for Fibrous Systems

Marshall Prado,
Moritz Dörstelmann



In the first half of the last century, the industrial revolution was well underway and the popularization of mass production had dramatically changed the culture of manufacturing and fabrication. Architecture in particular had become transfixed by the efficiency of standardization and serialized manufacturing. There was a tendency toward a machinic understanding of precision, measurability, and describability that has become engrained in the profession today. Material that was once transformed by the skillful hand of a master craftsman, with all the embedded knowledge of the material behaviour, capabilities, and techniques, was then uniformly processed and constrained to machines utilized for rapid production. This had a dramatic effect, not only on the construction processes of buildings but also on the process of architectural conception.

This was the ethos of the time and the climate in which fiber-reinforced polymers were first developed. Fabrication techniques developed for working with this material were characteristic of that agenda. They relied on formwork and molds that could be reused to make fibrous-composite copies of the desired geometry. As a substantial amount of material, cost, and time is devoted to the manufacturing of these surface molds, there is a natural inclination to reuse these molds to make multiple identical parts or risk even greater expense for manufacturing unique parts in which the molds would be discarded after only one use. Loose or matted fibers were hand-laid on these molds, impregnated with resin, and pressed to create a homogeneous material structure with a smooth, pressed, plastic-like finish. The formability of the material as well as the high strength-to-weight ratio allowed for a wide variety of surface geometries to be created and proved suitable for a wide variety of performance-driven engineering applications, such as the aerospace, automotive, and boat-building industries.

Since the introduction of fiber-reinforced polymers, many developments have been made which make these material systems suitable for architectural applications. The chemical composition of resin matrixes can be optimized to make the material stronger and more durable, vacuum-infusion techniques have increased the

2103 Research Project *fiber, force_FORM* by Tristan McGuire, Sunchung Min, Arthur Terry.

consistency of composite, and utilizing continuous fiber for mandrel-winding or pultrusion have increased the structural capacity of the fibrous system. The material is widely utilized in other industries yet the basic process of molding fiber-composites, however, has remained relatively unchanged. At the same time, technologies such as industrial robots and computational tools have developed, which have again changed the way we design and make. The robots are generic machines capable of being utilized for a wide variety of tasks, including fiber winding, and the computational tools can be used to negotiate the wide variety of design and fabrication criteria. Other than a few attempts to utilize these materials structurally, architecture has been unable to capitalize on fiber-reinforced polymers for their highly performative characteristics. Manufacturers take advantage of the formability of the material for surface panelling or lightness, as they have done in other industries, but disregard the inherent structural capacities of the material. The standard processes for manufacturing fiber-reinforced polymers, which remain almost unchanged from the development of the material system decades ago, do not meet the changing demands of the architectural-design field and the construction industry. These fields, which have changed considerably since the inception of fiber-reinforced polymers, have diverged from the uniform, machinic-industrialized paradigm, toward that which one might say is based on geometric variation, material resourcefulness, functional integration, and performative differentiation. This makes standard tectonic and fabrication practices outdated or irrelevant for current architectural applications. Therefore new fabrication techniques and design strategies are required to fully employ fiber-reinforced polymers in the building industry.

Research at the University of Stuttgart's Institute for Computational Design and Construction (ICD) and the Institute for Building Structures and Structural Design (ITKE) has focused in recent years on developing new fabrication and design processes for utilizing fiber-reinforced polymers. Coreless filament winding (CFW), a technique that requires no surface mold but rather the interaction of subsequently laid fibers to form a structured surface, is among the most promising techniques for creating composite structures for architectural applications. Since CFW requires no mold it is not tied to serialized production or limited by the use of superfluous material, it opens up new possibilities in architecture production and design. In parallel to the research at the University of Stuttgart, which has focused on developing these novel fabrication strategies and implementing them in large-scale architectural demonstrators, the fiber studios given by Achim Menges at the Harvard University Graduate School of Design were intended to further explore the design potentials in architecture that these processes enabled. In this way both fabrication and design could be simultaneously explored in various arenas to expose a wider range of processes and potentials within a shared subject matter and methodology. It is clear from these concurrent investigations that neither area of interest, fabrication or design strategies, can be explored in isolation but rather are interdependent. Form and formation are inherently linked to each other and require an understanding of material logics to be fully integrated into a design methodology.

As part of the Menges studio at the Harvard GSD from 2013 to 2015, a series of expert workshops were held. These workshops were intended to introduce the participating students to fibrous morphologies through a study of materials, processes, geometric investigations, and fabrication techniques. These are part of an integrative design process where material behavior and fabrication strategies become primary-design drivers. A bottom-up investigation into winding processes was utilized, allowing the students to explore fibers and matrixes as well as experimental techniques for constructing form. Through hand-winding experiments, moldless fabrication could be explored. This included the creation of various winding frameworks and the development of performative winding syntaxes—the sequential placement of fibers allow subsequent fiber to press on previous fibers, creating a composite surface without the need for a mold. Students could intuitively explore fiber patterns, surface generation, fiber interaction, and tension control in order to understand the specific parameters of coreless filament winding. The winding syntaxes can be expressed algorithmically, bridging the gap between material behavior and fabrication processes through computational design tools. This allowed morphologic studies, through the generation of curvature, to create structured surfaces and thickened fibrous bundles, not possible with surface molds, and the development of volumetric spaces with continuous fiber structures. On a material level, the orientations of the anisotropic fibers could be defined to program the structural behavior and increase the efficiency of the system by only placing fibers in orientations where they could be most effective and only in areas where material is needed. Using fabrication constraints as a filter, several of these design experiments were robotically fabricated in the workshops to understand how robotic limitations can further influence the design process. Students were introduced to basic robotic programming, strategies for digitally controlled winding, and the benefits of automated manufacturing.

These investigations are intended to explore the intricate relationship between tectonics and making, where form is not conceived in isolation and subsequently manufactured to specifications, but rather the form is derived from the process of fabrication. This could not be more true than for the generative winding strategies being developed in this studio, as form is not denoted by the dimensional designations of length, width, and height, but rather as the sequence in which the winding takes place. In the case of fibrous tectonics, structural conception shares a similar distinction from modernist tropes where assemblages of generic parts and functional separations are typical, but performance is rather constructed at the material level, where anisotropic system behaviours can be embedded in the arrangement of fibers. This challenges preconceived structural typologies and creates a novel architectural expression. Through the work of the studio and the related research at the University of Stuttgart, it has been shown that novel architectural systems can be developed from performative materials, systems, and processes.

Following page: Production photo from 2014 Research Project *Slack Systems* by Alice Chai, Nancy Nichols.

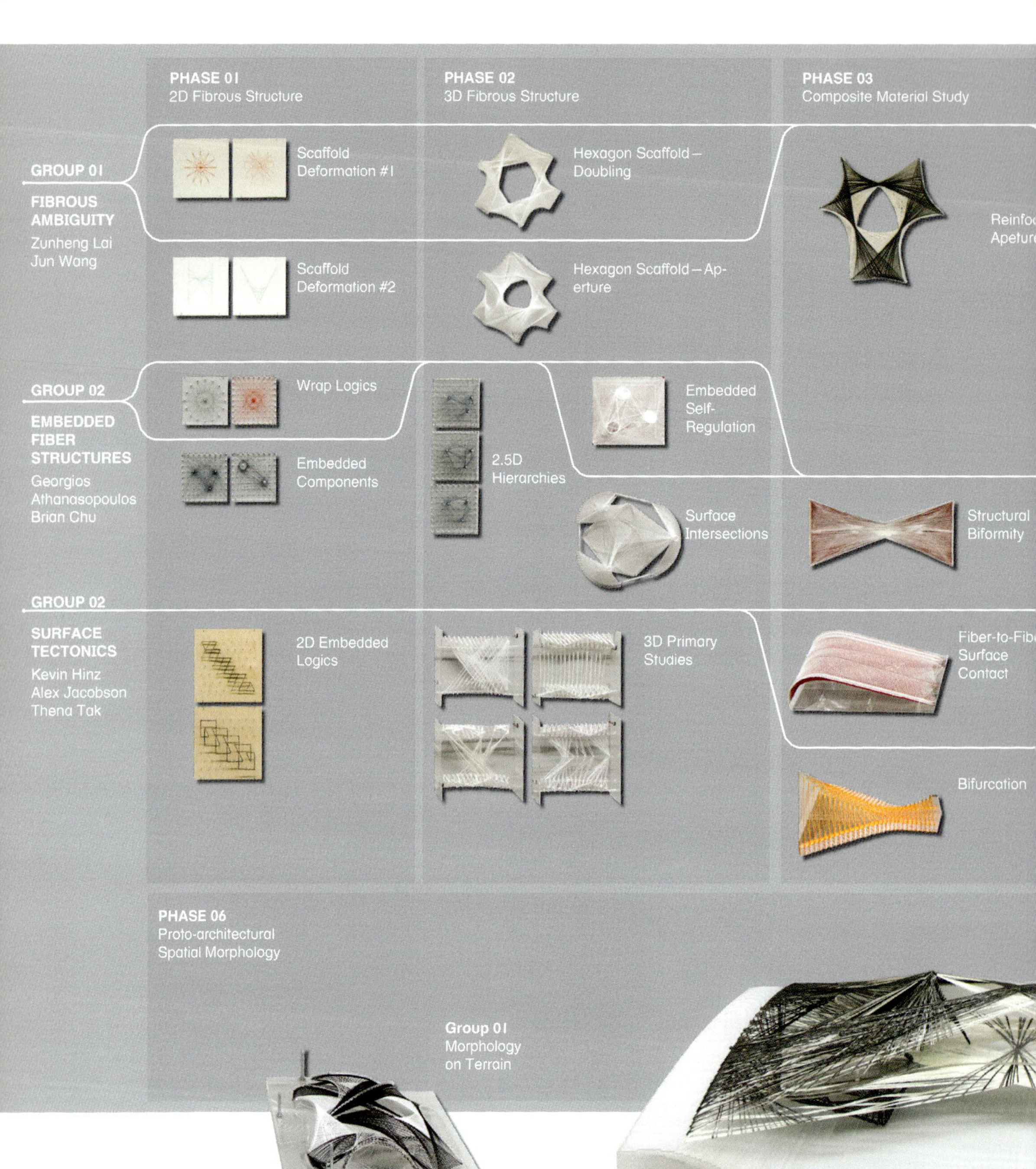


*Material Perfomances: Fibrous Tectonics*, January 27–March 23, 2014, Gund Hall, Harvard University Graduate School of Design. Rendering of exhibition display.

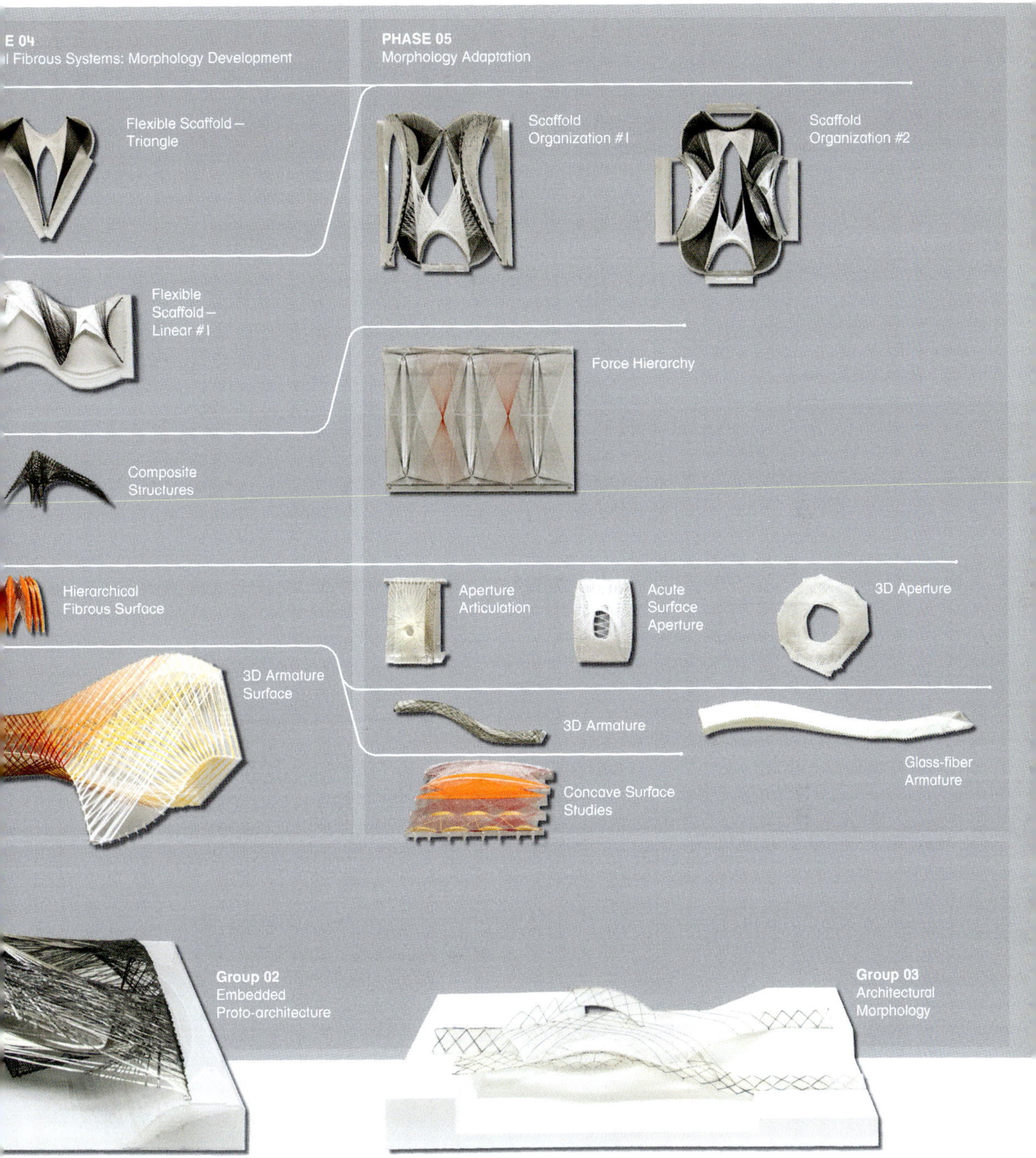

**E 04**
l Fibrous Systems: Morphology Development

**PHASE 05**
Morphology Adaptation

Flexible Scaffold – Triangle

Scaffold Organization #1

Scaffold Organization #2

Flexible Scaffold – Linear #1

Force Hierarchy

Composite Structures

Hierarchical Fibrous Surface

Aperture Articulation

Acute Surface Aperture

3D Aperture

3D Armature Surface

3D Armature

Glass-fiber Armature

Concave Surface Studies

**Group 02**
Embedded Proto-architecture

**Group 03**
Architectural Morphology

2013 Research Project *Fibrous Mandrel System* by Joon Hyuk Choe, Jeonghyun Kim, Rachel Moranis.

# Studio Projects

# Armature Surface

Kevin Hinz
Alexander Jacobson
Thena Tak



This research began with the assumption that New Materials are entitled to New Construction Logics. The study methodically investigates the inherent material properties specific to fibrous systems as applied to a continuous structure of interconnected fibrous surfaces. The research trajectory begins with 2D-pattern studies, integrating an internal logic of fiber build-up before progressing into a three-dimensional structure of armatures and spanning surfaces as an integrated system. The goal is to investigate the attributes of fibrous tectonics to create New Spatial Morphologies.

Our studies focus on the development of a 2D-fiber-distribution system embedded with an internal logic. Our team resisted a traditional approach, we wanted to develop a fiber form inherent to the material system. An internal logic was determined by a three to five step algorithm that defined points around which we would wrap a single fiber string. Subsequent steps would build fiber density to approximate more developed 3D structures exposed in later research. This family of algorithms, called a series of linksets, was always terminated at a different point than where it began. This ensured that the algorithm would not build up fiber in a single location, but would also define a global movement of fiber placement throughout the grid according to the applied algorithm. Constraints included the container in which the script operated, and unexpected looping of the pattern according to its mathematical origin and set of operations. The internal logic was initially a success, however it was apparent that more control of a global form would be required to evolve from a two-dimensional system to a three-dimensional structural form.

Planar systems do not support positive three-dimensional fiber-to-fiber interaction. By integrating the linkset definition with the trajectory of a free-form line, the three-dimensional architectural discourse could evolve into an a more complex set of surface structures. Simple 2D extrusions, used initially as scaffolding techniques, revealed the three-dimensional potential of the original linkset. However, fiber-to-fiber contact was limited and spatial attributes were non-existent. The link had to become an autonomous, spatially uninhibited element. Dimensional characteristics were achieved by introducing a Z-Axis dimension to the linkset algorithm, which later resulted in the fiber armature. The system retained a local internal logic with dimensional characteristics.

The initial linkset of fiber of embroidery thread would be wrapped around a temporary acrylic scaffold before being embedded with epoxy resin. This became an armature around which subsequent fibrous surfaces could be wrapped. It was necessary to harden the armature before subsequent wrapping to create a rigid element that resisted applied tensile forces of the fibrous surface structure. Once the armature and subsequent surface structures were wrapped, the entire system was again emerged in the epoxy matrix resulting in a continuous fibrous tectonic. These assembly techniques became a palette of fibrous strategies deployed as tectonic strategies.

Scaffolding was an important construction system that inevitably guided fibrous form and determined the final spatial morphology. We elected to develop a model of constructing sweeps along a curve that moved freely in three dimensions, requiring a support system. A wide variety of scaffolding offered varying degrees of 3D movement, various states of structural rigidity, and the ability to bifurcate armatures. Bifurcation was particularly important for introducing growth and tectonic continuity into the system. Scaffolding connections had to be loose-fitting to adapt to the tensile forces later introduced by the fibrous lay-up (rigid connections caused unpredictable breakage). Control over the spacing of the fiber lay-up (placement of scaffold), the curvature of the armature, and the global geometry of the system allowed for a construction logic that investigated surface construction, fiber-to-fiber interaction, and articulation of structural fibrous-surfaces.

The curvature between armatures determines the ability to cinch fibers onto each other. Convex curvature allowed fiber-to-fiber interaction to be controlled with a modification to the "skip" (the number of spacing increments between scaffolding) within the wrapping algorithm. Achieving fiber-to-fiber contact with concave curvature is difficult because it requires the use of complex cinching techniques from a secondary scaffold, or the application of irregular, seemingly erratic wrapping algorithms, to ensure surface structures. Nevertheless, these relationships were manageable if the concavity was not too acute nor abutted by relatively severe convex areas of the scaffold.

The degree of curvature is closely related to the algorithmic skip size. The skip spacing also dictates the number of fibers that build up at points on the scaffolding. When the scaffolding is curved, the skipping logic results in ridges of concentrated fiber. The team constructed an analytical tool which made it possible to investigate sequencing in the wrapping process. The computer-run algorithm first identified a maximum "wrap-able" envelope defining a base layer of fiber for a given set of scaffolds. Second, the script identified structural wrapping patterns that added fiber density to the system before the application of a final set of cinching patterns, which offered additional rigidity and concentrated fiber buildup. By combining a study of various wrapping techniques with the varying degree impacts of curvature with algorithmic skipping, an informed hierarchical distribution of surface articulation was introduced.

The algorithm for wrapping is not limited to surface structures. Wrapping patterns can articulate apertures. Our investigations began with a curve that defined an opening before mapping the tangents to said curve. We allowed these tangents to determine the spacing increments on the armature, much like the initial 2D investigations used the algorithm to determine points for fiber placement. This technique results in a dense buildup of fiber around the opening of the aperture perpendicular to the direction in which cracks were likely to propagate in homogeneous structural surfaces. We studied the steps necessary to articulate apertures of multiple sizes, and degrees of lateral displacement.

With a system of fibrous construction logics, the final stage examined spatial morphologies. The result incorporated four bifurcating armatures, yielding an interconnected framework to support structural surfaces. In cross-section, one armature has a diameter large enough and a bottom flat enough to become an occupy-able tube-like enclosure. Another has a wide sectional profile and a flat top to resist lateral bending and function as a pathway. A third armature serves as structural support, providing convex curvature necessary to ensure surface structure. The final armature responds to the other three, allowing for head-height above the pathway and adjusting in profile to accommodate ideal fiber-to-fiber surface armature lamination.

This research offers the possibility of constructing complex fibrous structures in a two-phase process. Multiple armatures are constructed using acrylic scaffolding with subsequent fibrous surfaces wrapped between armatures. Future areas of inquiry might include an investigation into surface articulation with fiber buildup and layering, further exploiting the benefits of the material system.

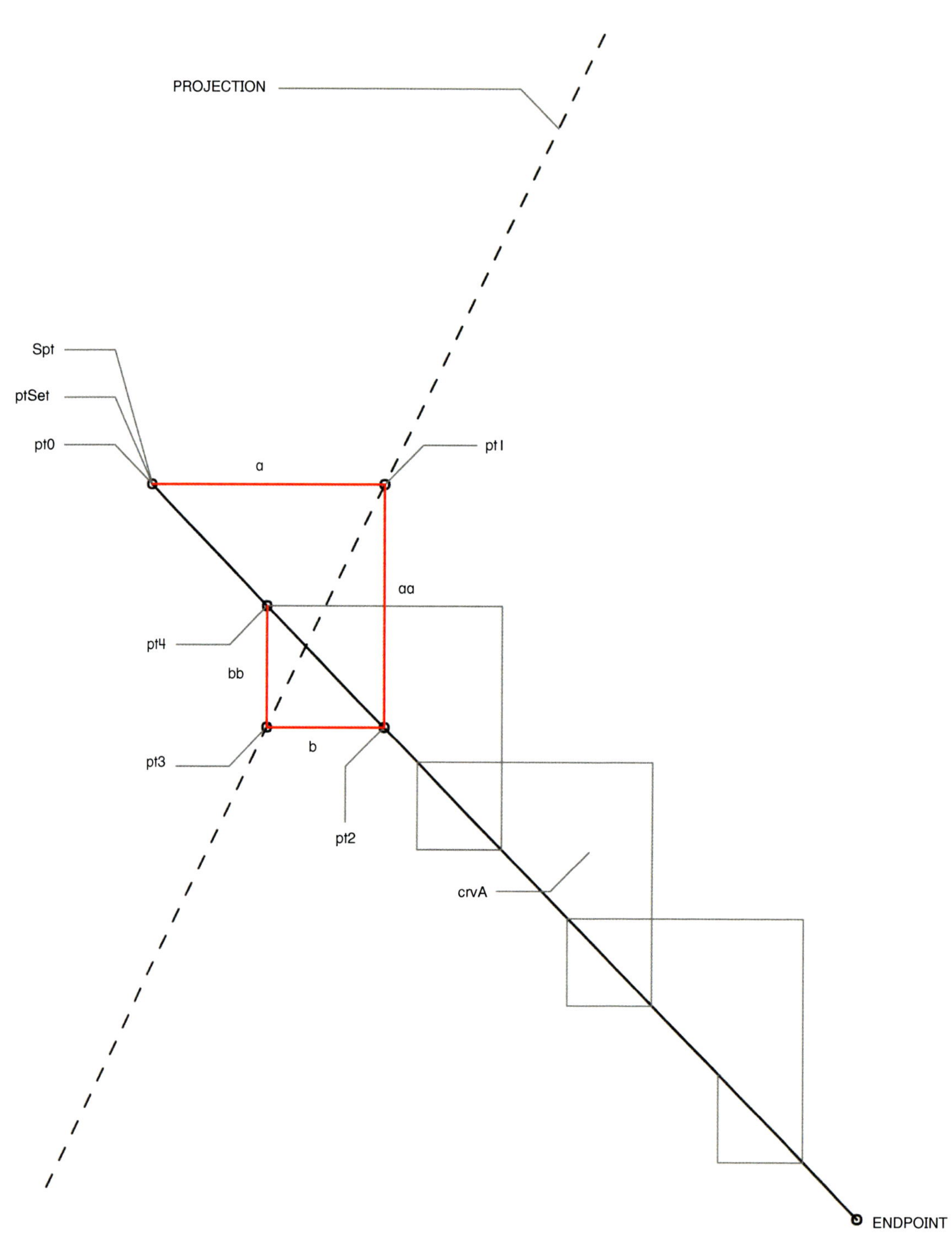
PROJECTION
Spt
ptSet
pt0
a
pt1
aa
pt4
bb
pt3
b
pt2
crvA
ENDPOINT

CODE SCRIPT

```
set new point to old point
  move new point an increment
    relative to input crv
  get pt1, add pt to output list

set new point to old point
  move new point an increment
    relative to input first fiber
  get pt2

set new point to old point
  move new point an increment
    relative toto input first fiber
  get pt3

set new point to old point
  move new point an increment
    rrelative to second and third fibers
  get pt4
create line[pt3,pt1]

modify changing variable
reset loop
```

INPUTS

cvrA: drive curves
permA: perimeter curv (tentative)
snail: limit loop length
q: ?
div: evaluation parameter for cvrA
input: upper limit for link modifier
r: evaluation variable, application of aa

VARIABLES

```
(a)
   where: a = ((Math.Abs(Ept.X) – Math.Abs(Spt.X)) / div);
(aa)
   modifier for line[pt1,pt2]
   where aa = (formula * (-1.0));
(aa1)
   where: aa1 = (a * 1.5);
   loop modified variable, dummy for (aa)
(b)
   where: b = Math.Abs(a * 0.5);
(bb)
   where: bb = c + (0.05 * (i));
  NOTE: this exprssion offers high degree of change
(c)
   dummy variable, initially 0
when: bb = c + (0.05 * (i));
   where c is initially set to zero
   (i) is used to step the change
formula: formula = Math.Sin(aa1);
   an expression used to change aa in relationship to a
```

Internal logic definition of linkset with algorithmic logic of filament directionality and geometry.

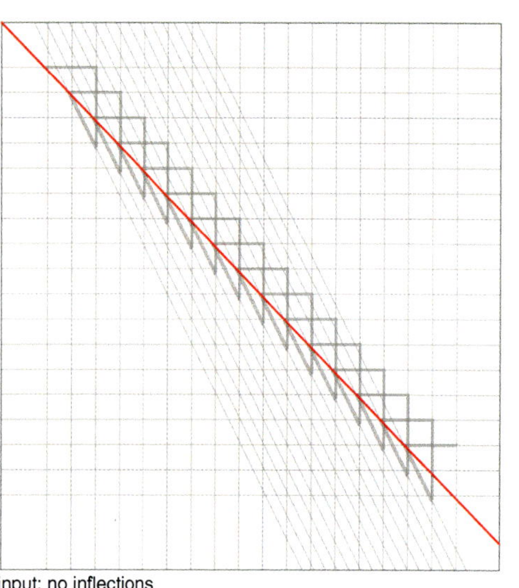

input: no inflections

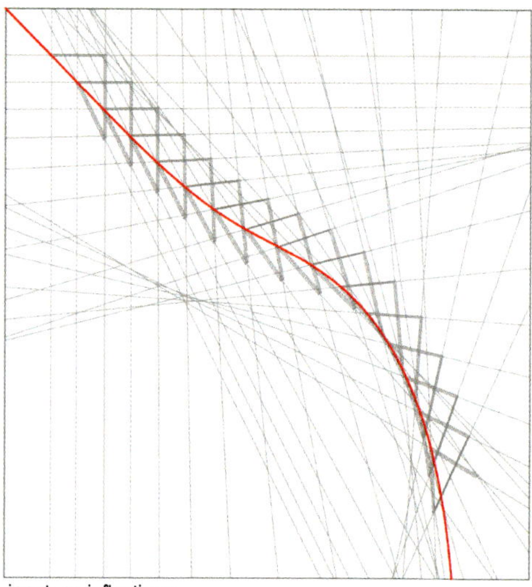

input: no inflections

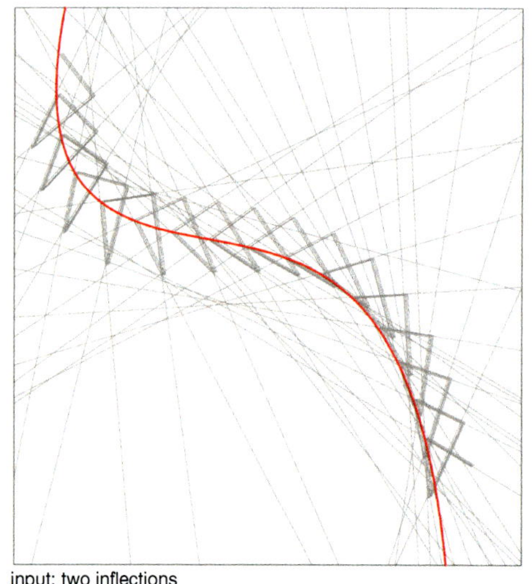

input: two inflections

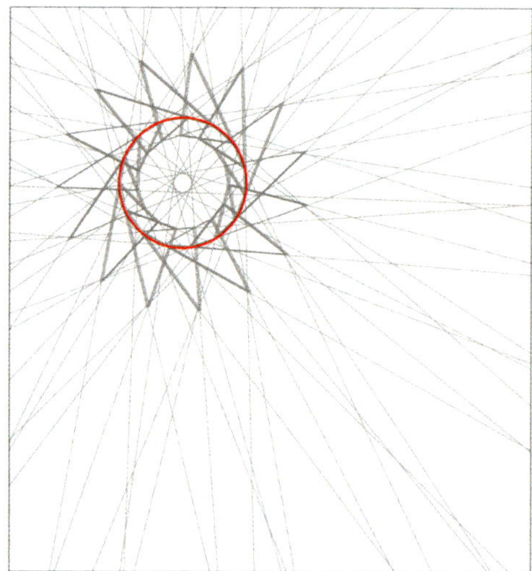

input: closed curve

Input curve variation and responsive quality of linkset.

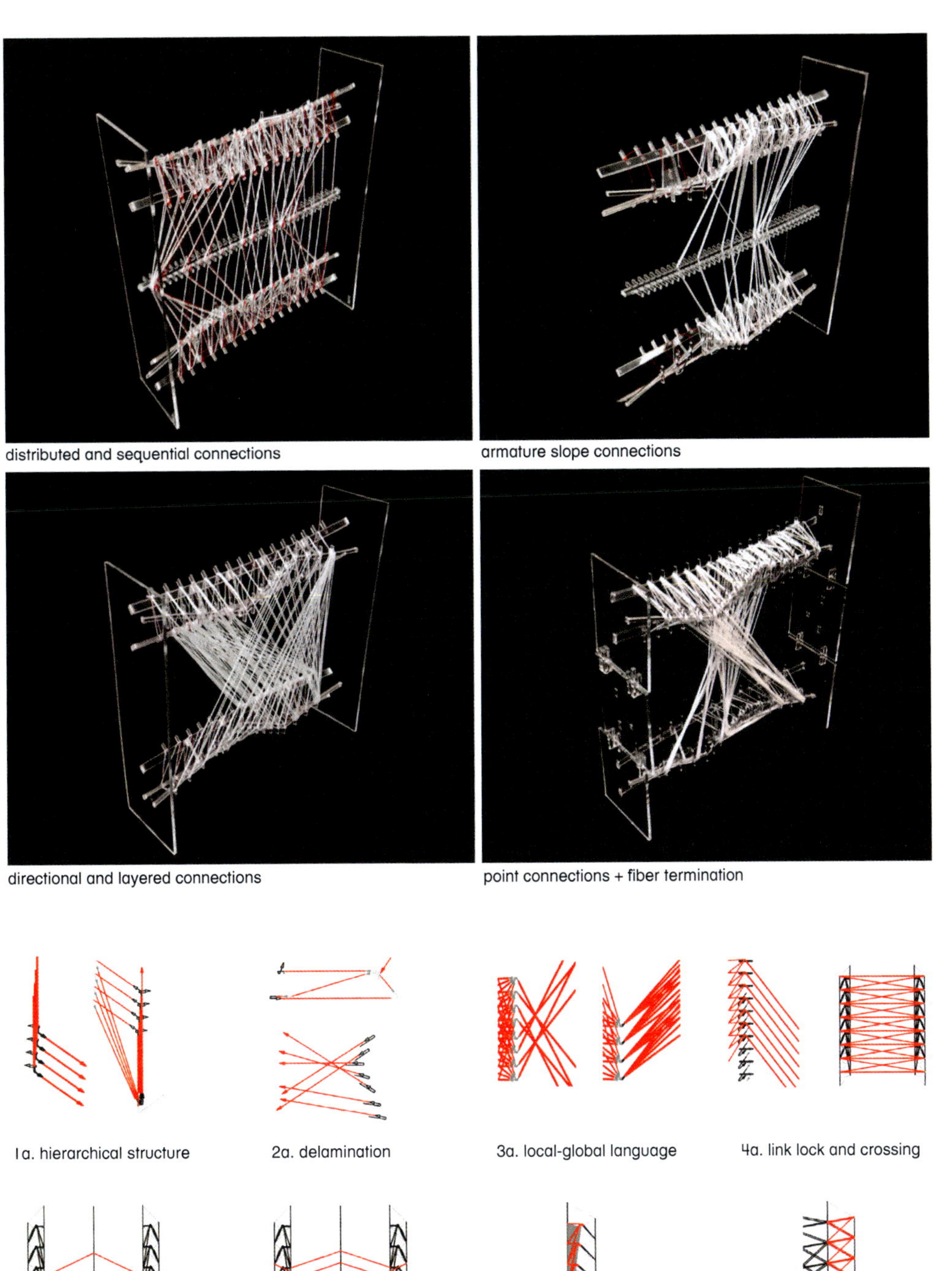

distributed and sequential connections

armature slope connections

directional and layered connections

point connections + fiber termination

1a. hierarchical structure

2a. delamination

3a. local-global language

4a. link lock and crossing

1b. comb-crossing link

2b. comb-addition of mass

3b. single sided hierarchy

4b. comb-crossing extension

Top: Principal study models showing armature-surface relationships, scaffolding technique, and fiber distribution.

Bottom: Index of wrapping techniques, logic, and methodology relative to each pricipal model.

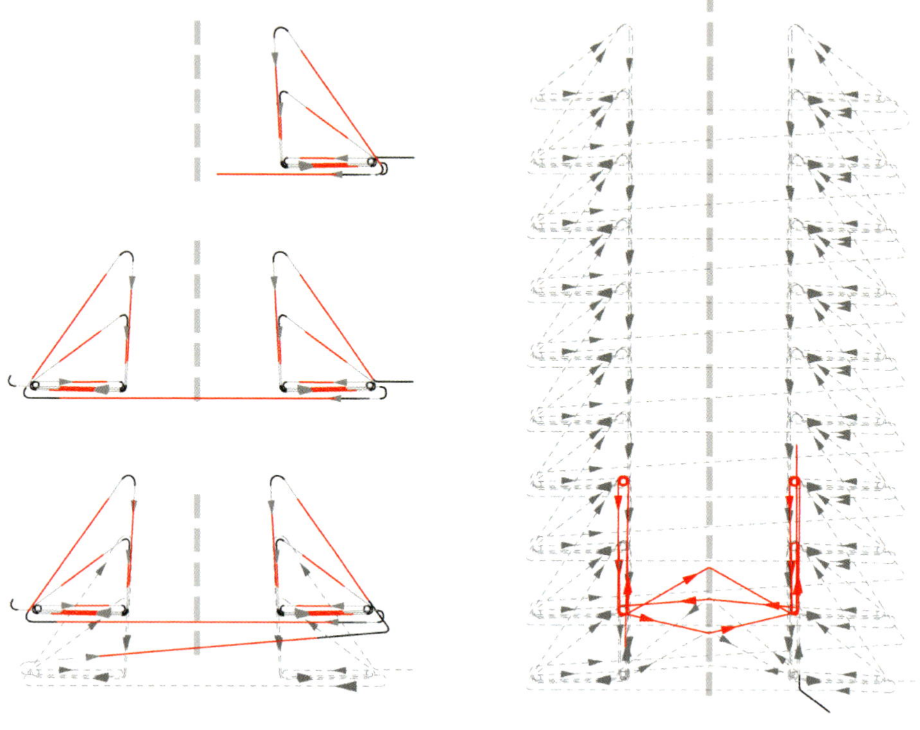



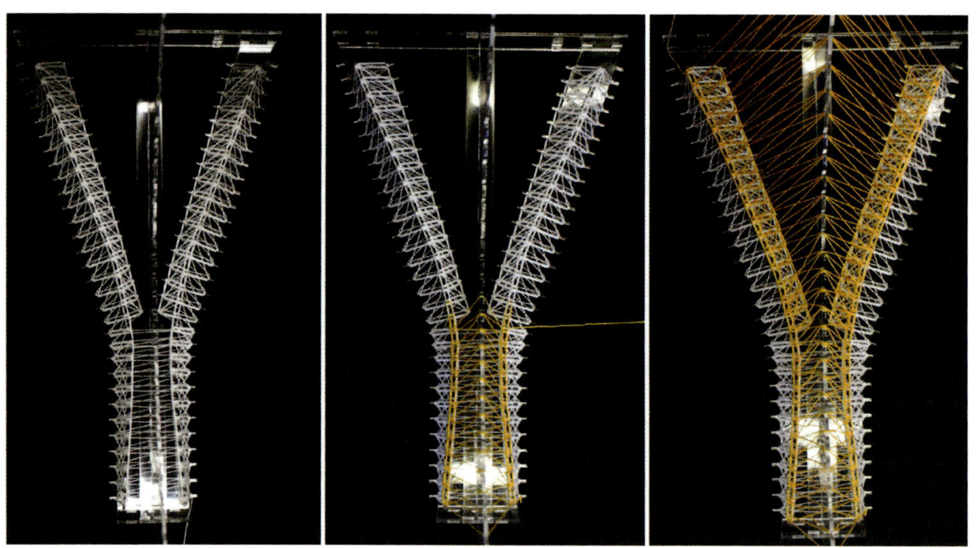



Top: Diagram of spatial development of surface armature with extraction and application of learned methods and techniques.

Bottom: The bifurcation methodology of sequencing wrapping continuous fiber as system bifurcates.

Following page: Model of spatial development of surface armature with extraction and application of learned methods and techniques.

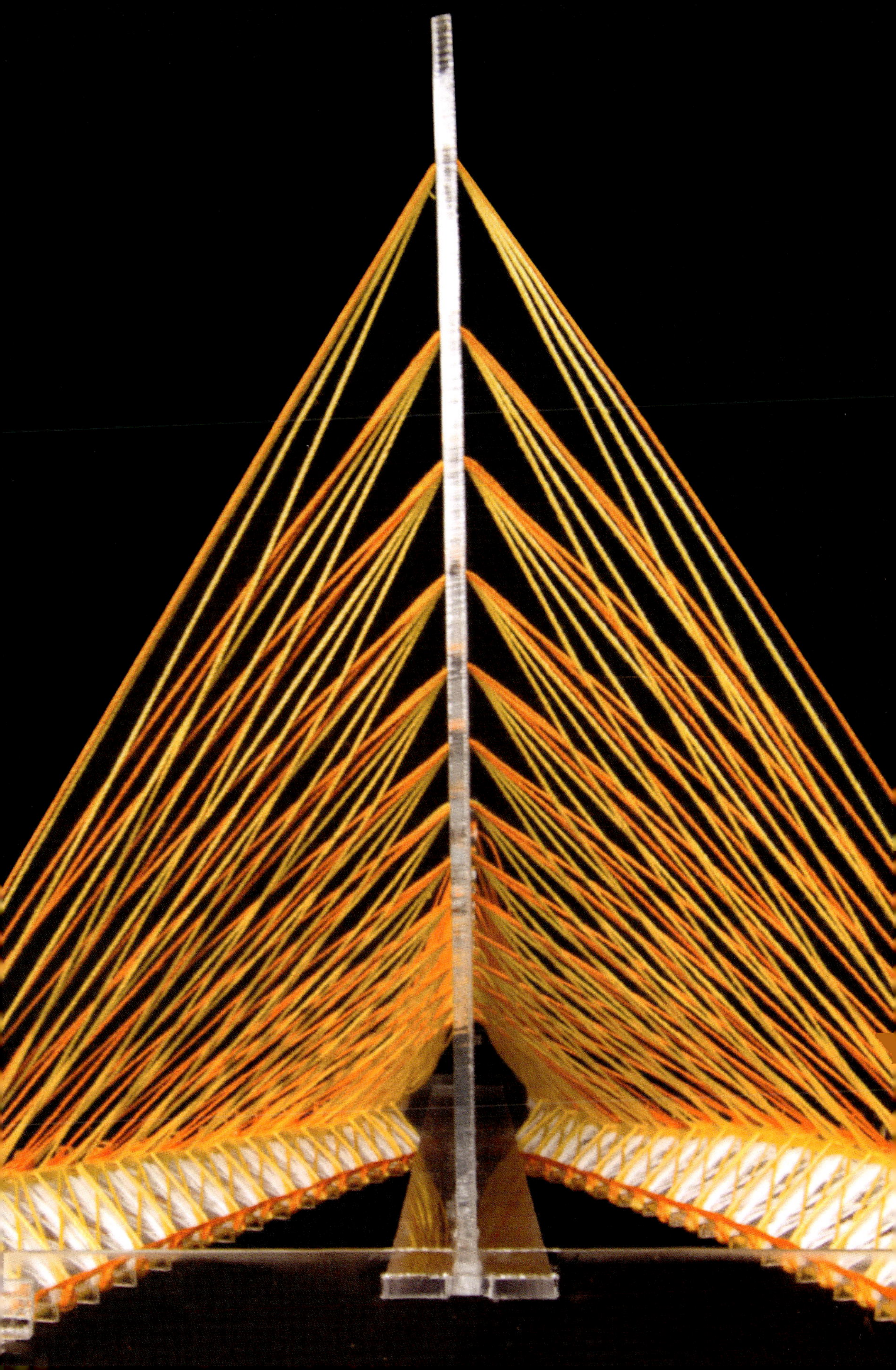

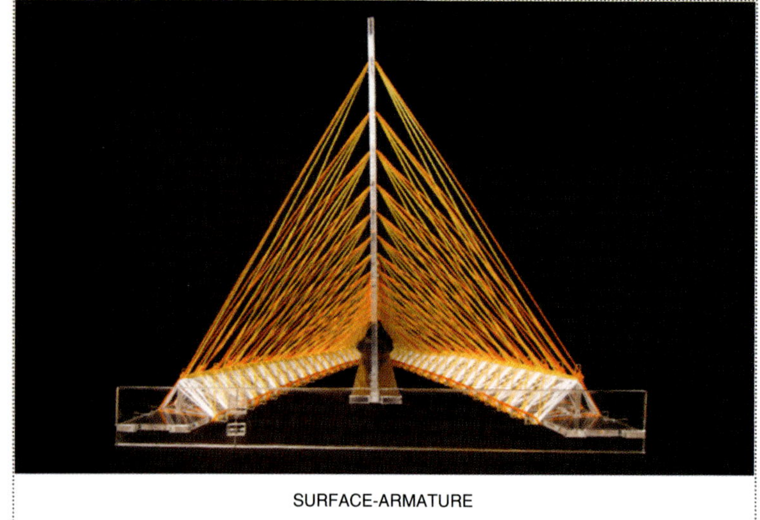

SURFACE-ARMATURE



Surface-armature model cataloging the studies generated after intial model.

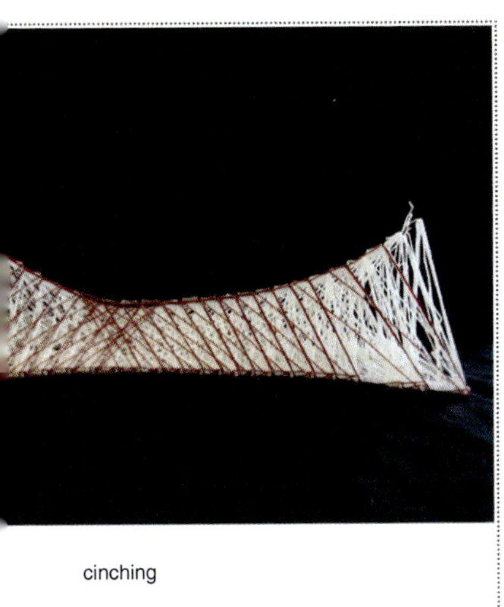

cinching

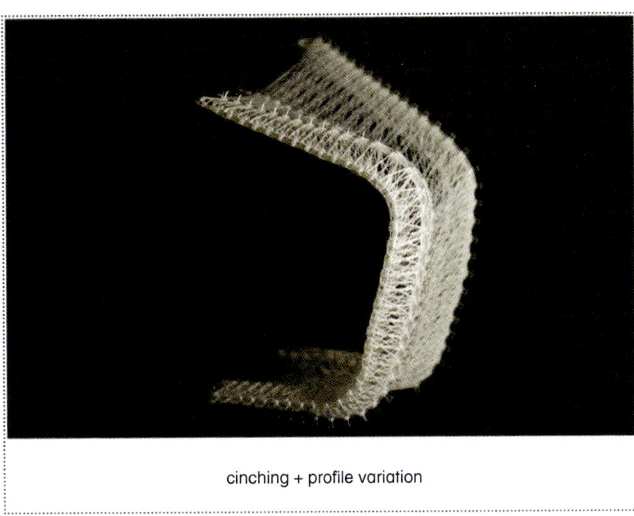

cinching + profile variation



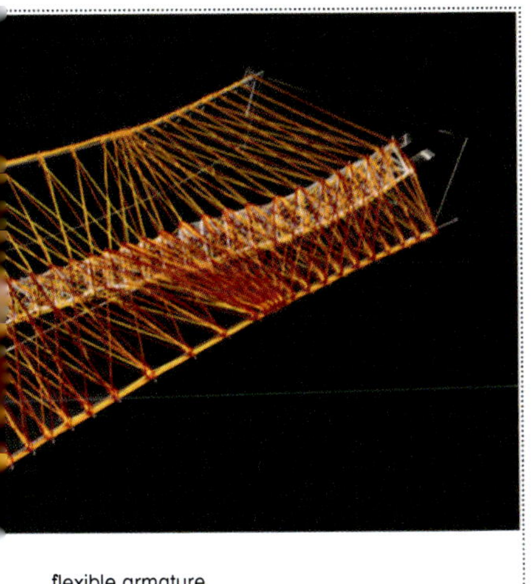

flexible armature

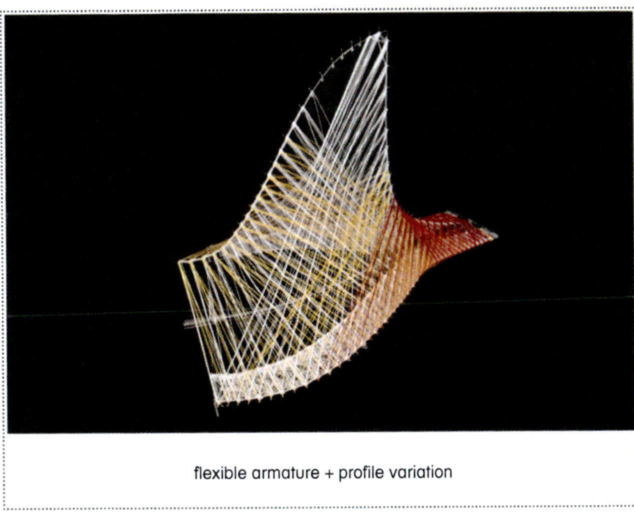

flexible armature + profile variation

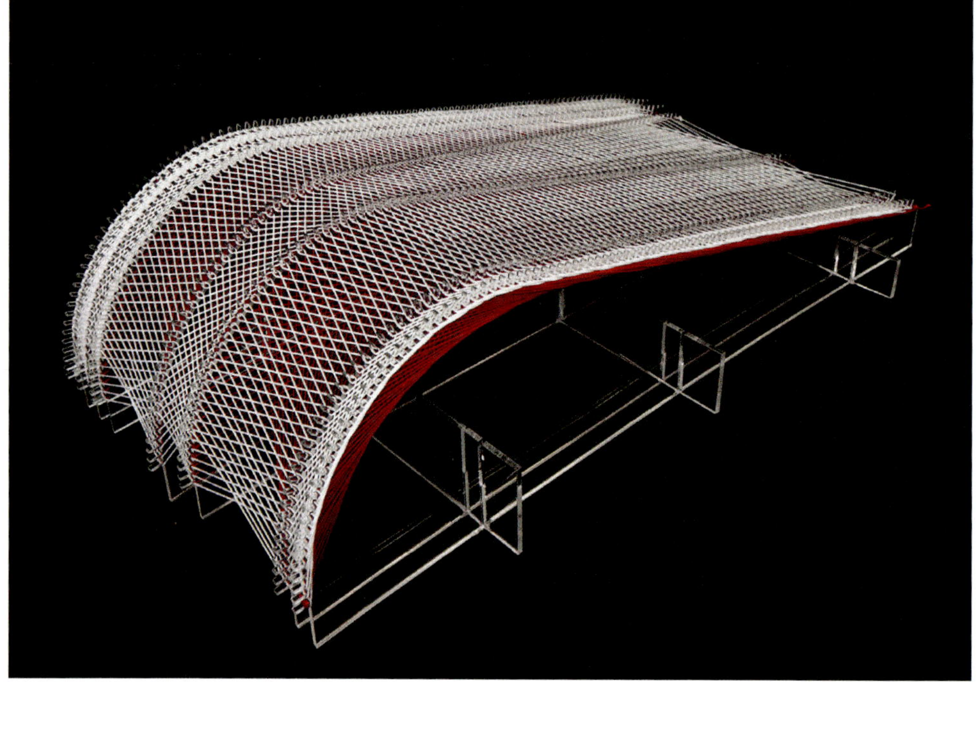

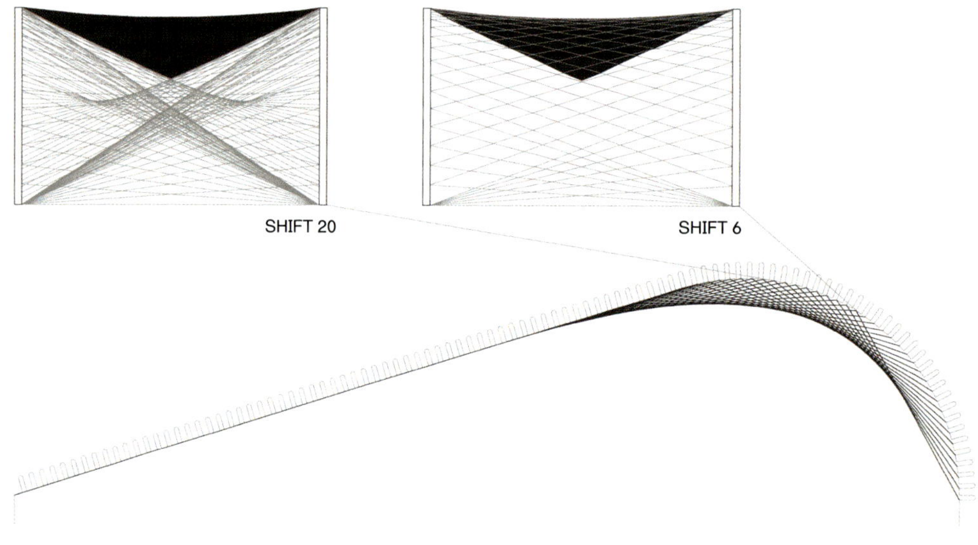


Top: Surface-armature model showing skipping technique that allows for fiber-to-fiber contact and structural depth.

Bottom: Wrapping logic and cinching technique of varied skipping produces fiber-to-fiber contact and structural depth.

Following page: Detail of surface-armature model showing skipping techique.

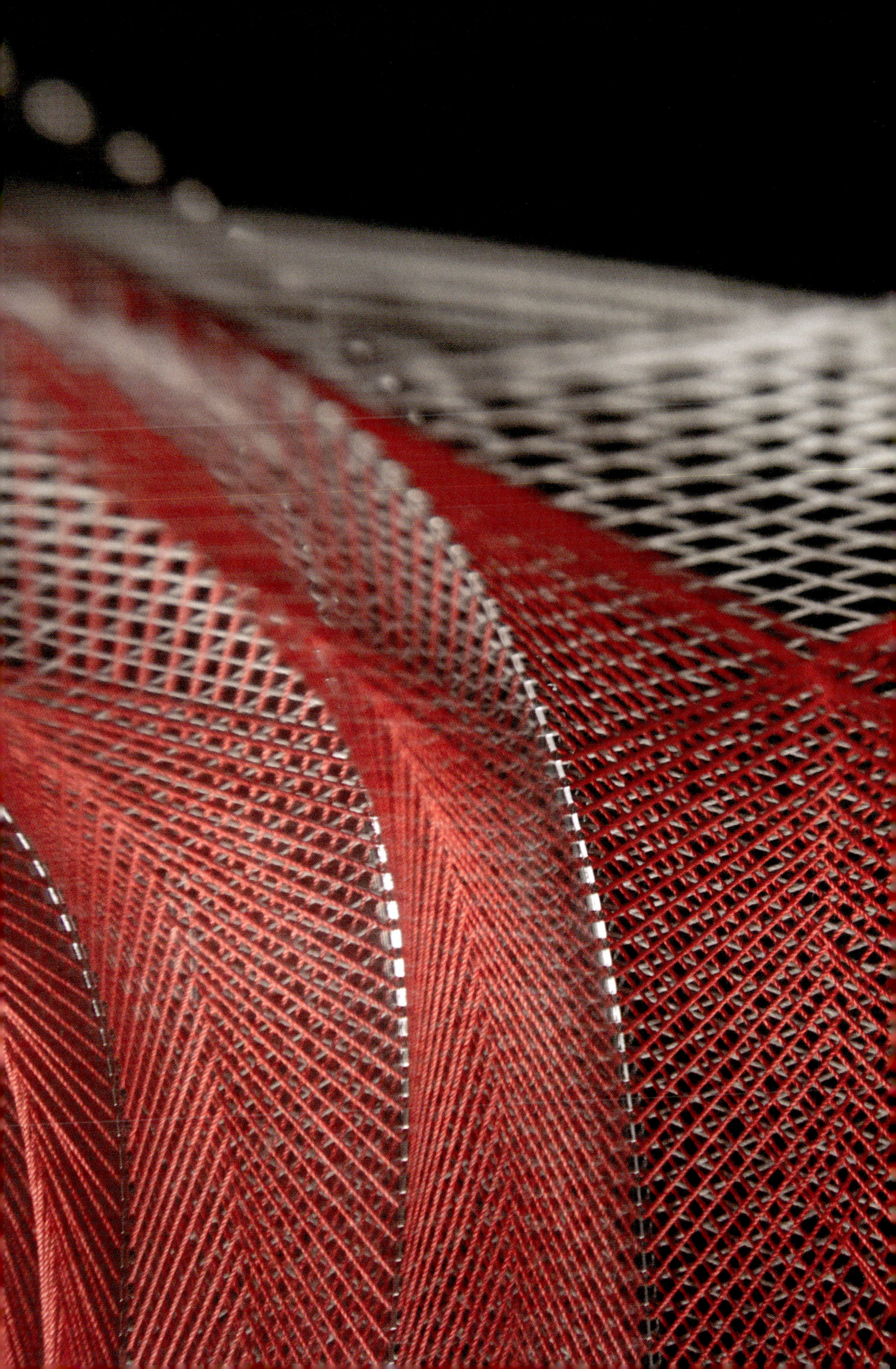

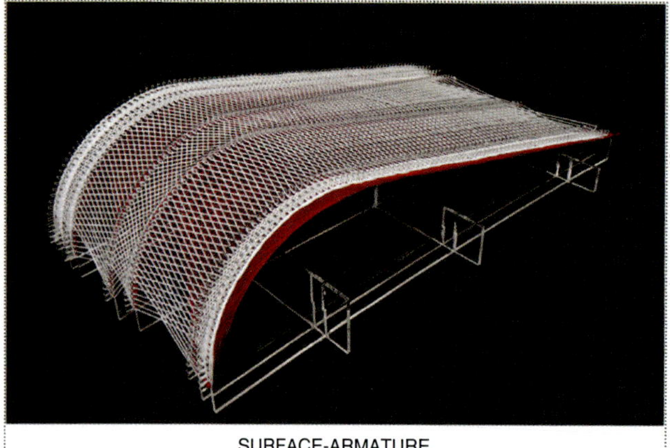
SURFACE-ARMATURE

propagation



Catalog of studies generated after intial
surface-armature model.

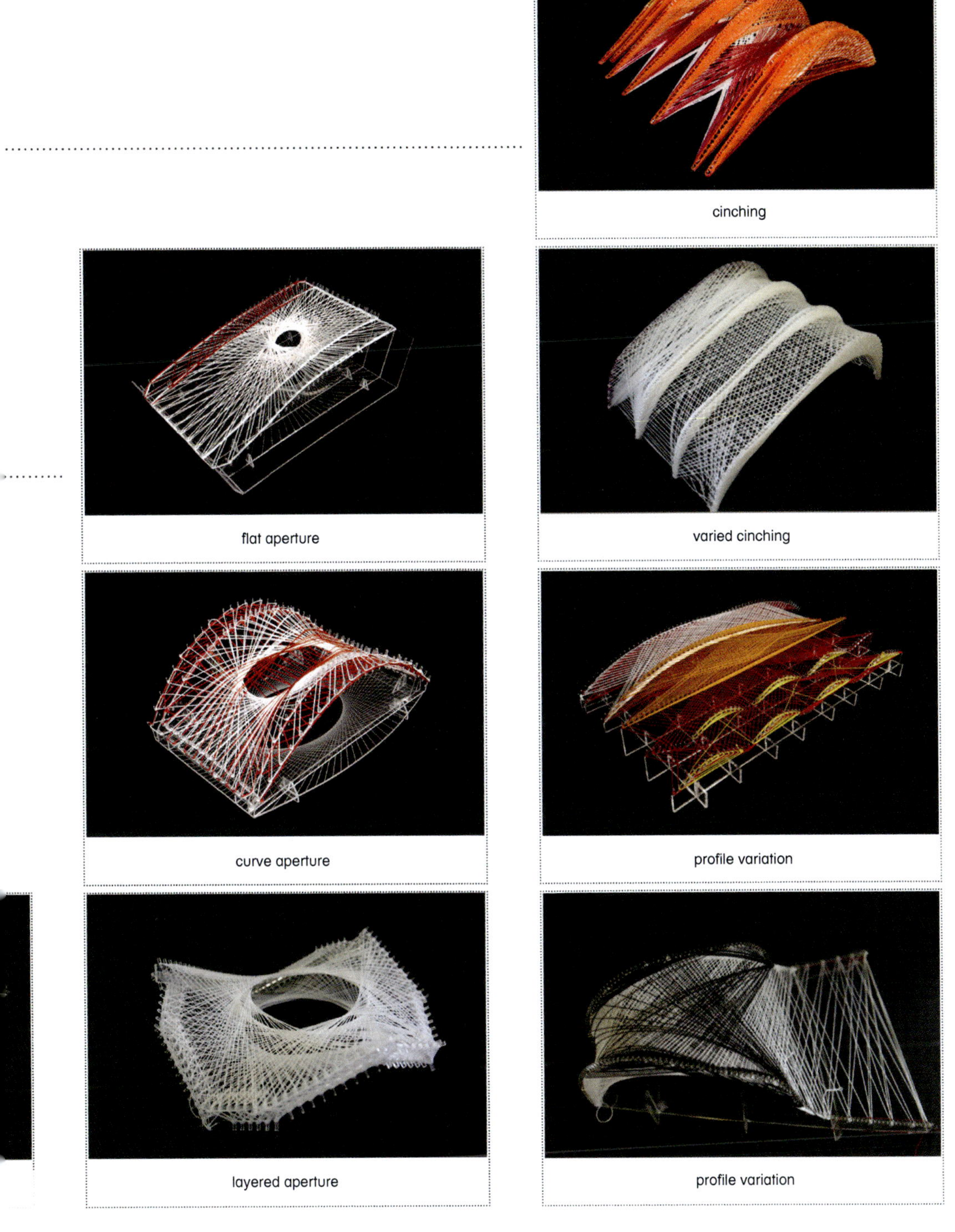

cinching

flat aperture

varied cinching

curve aperture

profile variation

layered aperture

profile variation

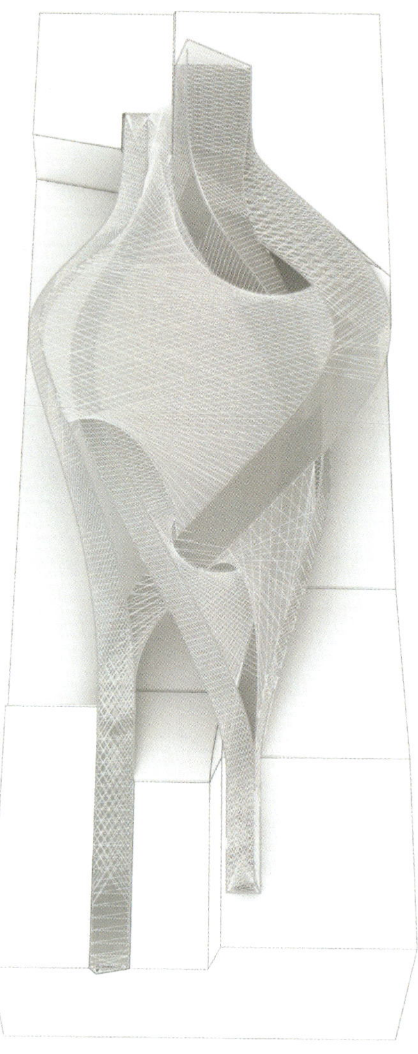

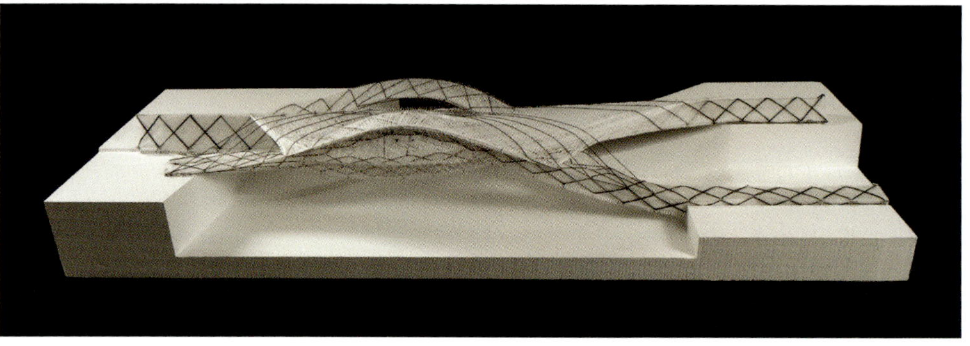

Top: Spatial-morphology elements of armature and surfaces.

Bottom: Spatial-morphology model.

Top and bottom: Perspective views within spatial-morphology model.

# Fiber Space Reciprocities

Georgios Athanasopoulos
Brian Chu



The project's primary attempt was to challenge conventional tectonics through the inspiration from biology and the fundamental principles of fibers distribution. In order to achieve that, the project was also oriented toward computational design methods, not only for purposes of simulation, but as a way to apply computation tools in order to pursue simple algorithmic logics that would reflect fiber-distribution patterns.

As a starting point of critique and in order to introduce an initial architectural hypothesis, the group focused on tensile and membrane structures. The reason for that was their ability to cover large openings and their qualities as light structures in general. The most important finding was the idea that these structures require a wide range of additional structural components in order for them to function properly and bear the required loads. For instance, tensile structures are based on a series of supplementary components such as nodes, additional cables that work in tension, as well as sizable steel masts. That particular investigation lead to a crucial inquiry of how an architectural morphology that would be based on fibrous tectonics could avoid any additional structural element and embody all structural components into one system. This would become the primary design principle for the entire project, the creation of an algorithmic system of fiber distribution capable of incorporating all the parts that are necessary for its consistency and stability.

The most important aspect regarding fiber distribution in nature would be their capacity to transform all the forces that they receive into tension instead of compression. This can happen through their continuity as well as through the interactions that happen among them. Another guiding principle for the project was to achieve as many fiber-to-fiber interactions as possible.

The first stage of experimentation was based on the construction of two-dimensional models that would obey simple algorithmic patterns in order to enhance the number of interactions between fibers. The patterns of investigation were based on a circle, a grid, and a boundary with internal points scaffolds. An important finding was the fact that as the fibers were laid, the result had three-dimensional properties and created space, even if the scaffolds were two-dimensional. Additionally, at that particular stage, the group discovered the opportunity of including scaffold components that at the end were embedded through the configuration of the fibers.

The next step was to shift the previous two-dimensional fiber articulations to a series of two-and-a-half-dimensional studies by moving the internal generated points on the vertical (z) axis. By doing so, there was the opportunity to include more than one layer of fiber-distribution patterns. This introduced a level of hierarchy between primary structural fiber-distribution layers and secondary systems. The principle of embedded components was once more explored through the secondary systems of articulation and thus gave the opportunity to create a series of aperture-like elements.

However the most important finding through the experiments was the idea to include three-dimensional embedded components between the hierarchical layers of fibers. The achievement was to introduce compression elements between the several layers of fibers that would force the one layer of fibers down. This lead to the establishment of self-determined surfaces as the result of the fibers under pressure.

Another set of studies tried to focus on the idea of intersecting planes that could come as a result from the winding patterns. By the term "surface," what is implied is the hypothetical epiphany that is created from parallel or common ending-fibers. The intersecting planes were conceived as a strategy that would offer high-architectural qualities. This investigation lead to the final distribution pattern of the fibers which would result in the proto-architectural morphology of the project.

As a next step, the aim was to follow the idea of the embedded components within the winding patterns. The result was the construction of a series of "pillar-like" structural components that would be constructed independently and added to the structure between the different layers of fibers. The role of these components would be to receive the compression forces of the fibers that, indeed, were in tension. The "pillar-like" components would generate an area around their base that was perceived as inhabitable space. An additional series of "pillar-like" components would be reversed in order to support the entire prototype to the ground.

As a next step, the aim was to create a sequence of the prototype architectural morphology. The goal was to articulate an architectural configuration that would be adaptable to its environment and at the same time redefine its surroundings. At that point, a series of additional architectural criteria were introduced, such as points of entrance, circulation paths, and vertical circulation systems. According to the length of the "span" structure, the distribution of fibers would change its density at particular areas and, in that way, it would provide different levels of translucency to the interior space. Additionally, secondary layers of fibers now could be articulated between the prototypes, and thus upgrade the complexity of the entire structure.

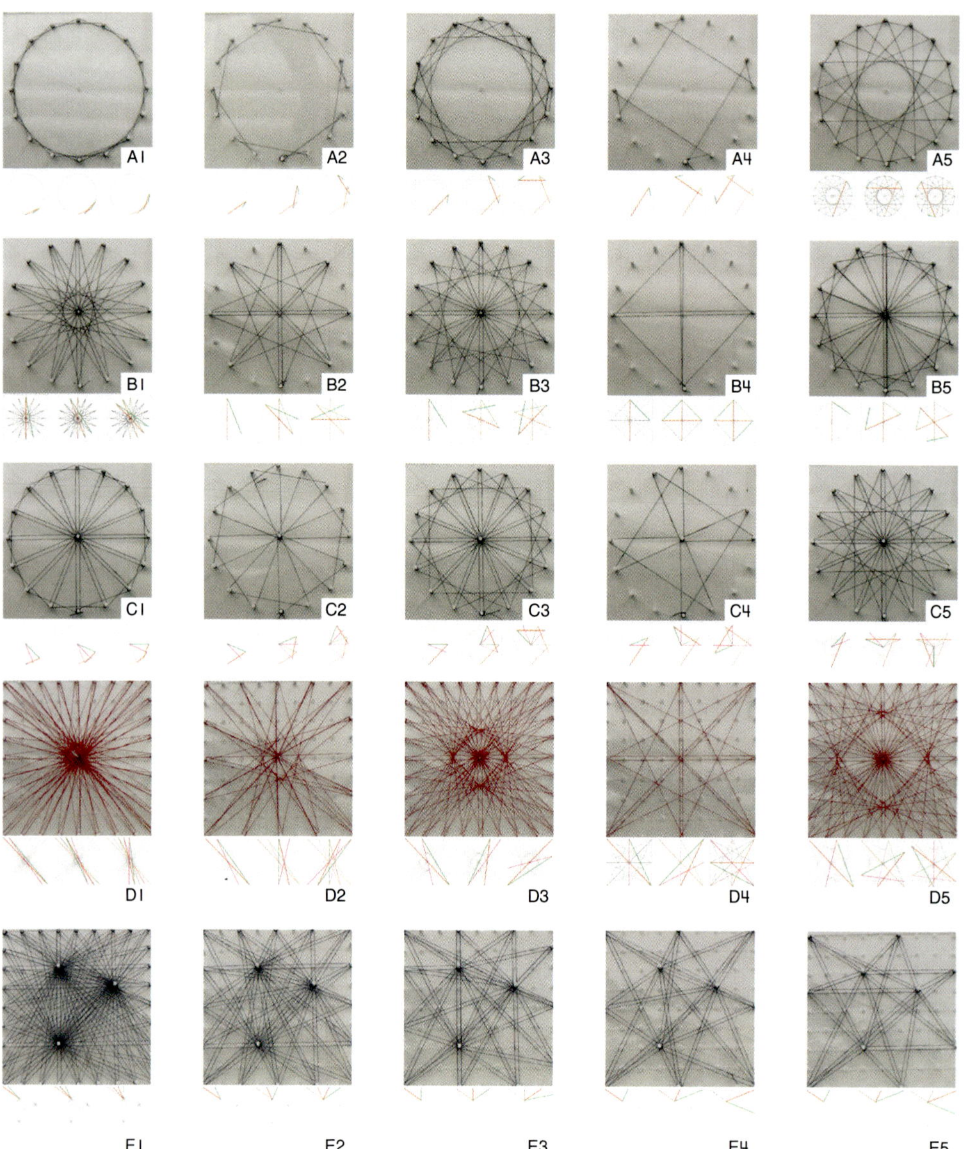


Matrix of two-dimensional winding studies.

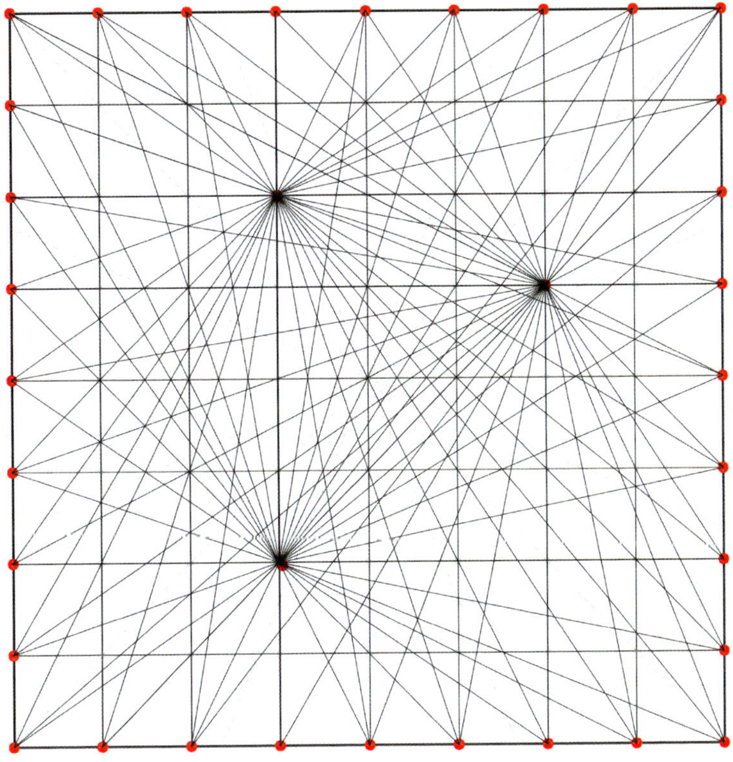

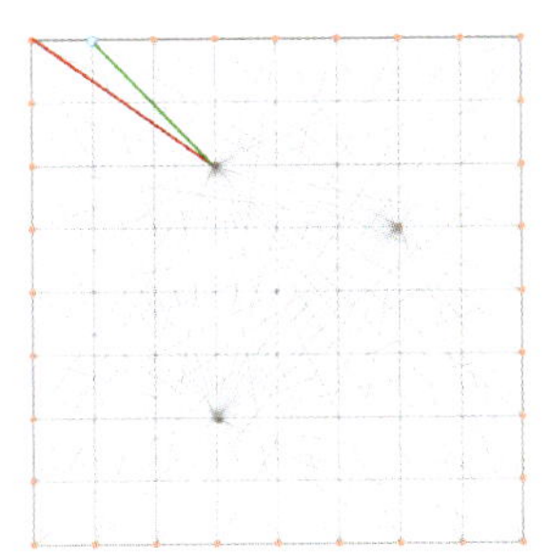

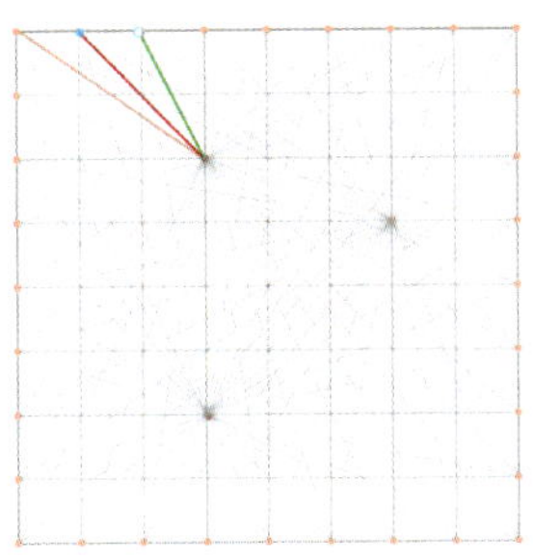

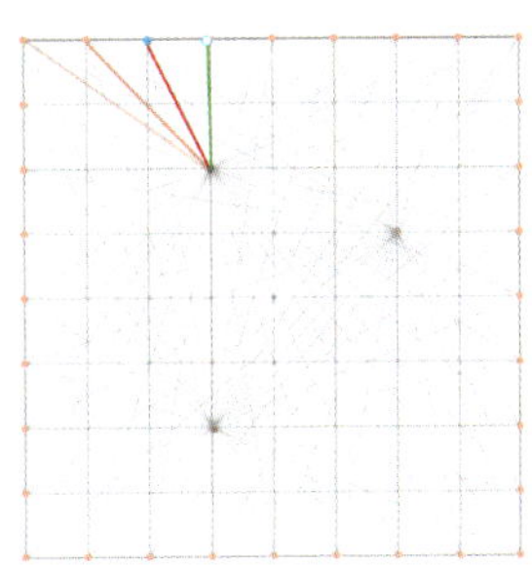

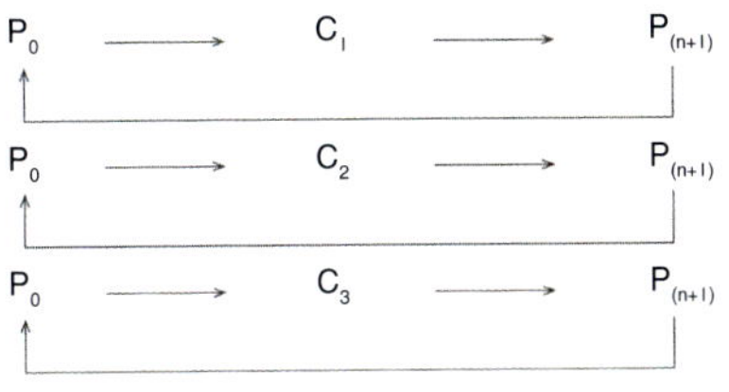


End Condition

Reach the first starting point

Algorithmic explorations of winding patterns.

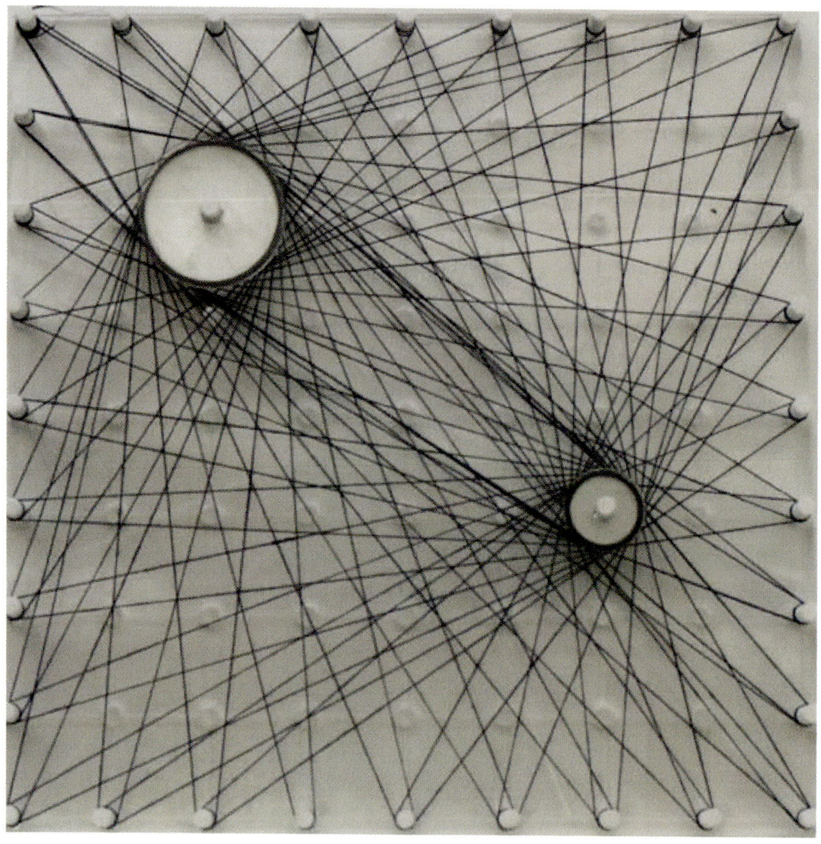

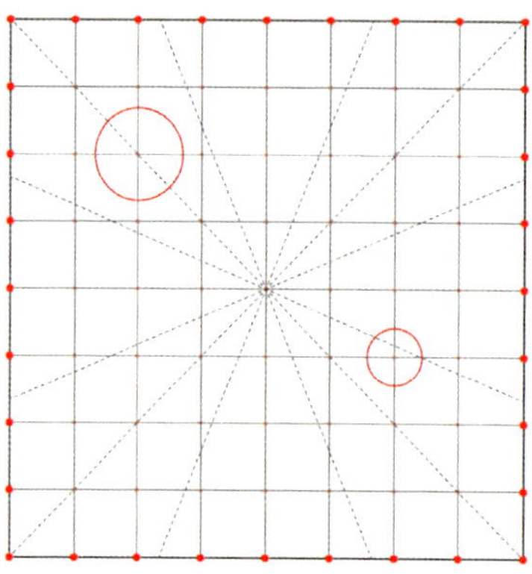

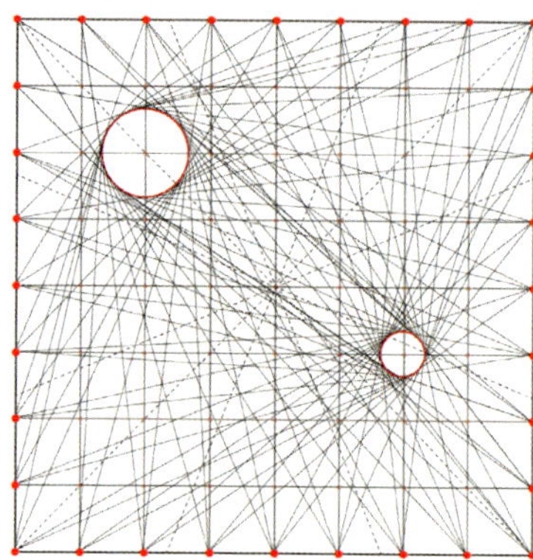

Above and following page: Models and studies of layered, embedded elements.

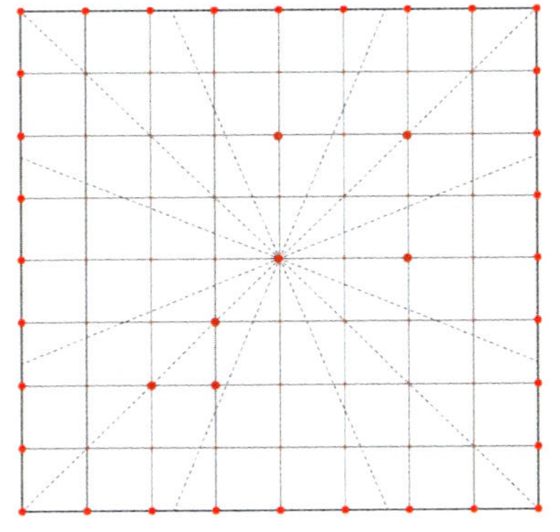

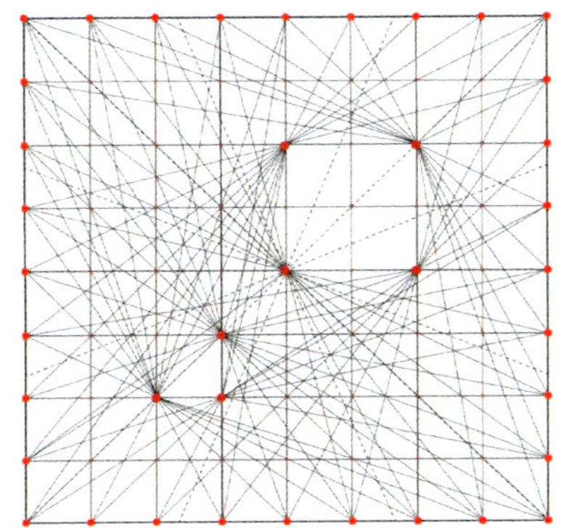

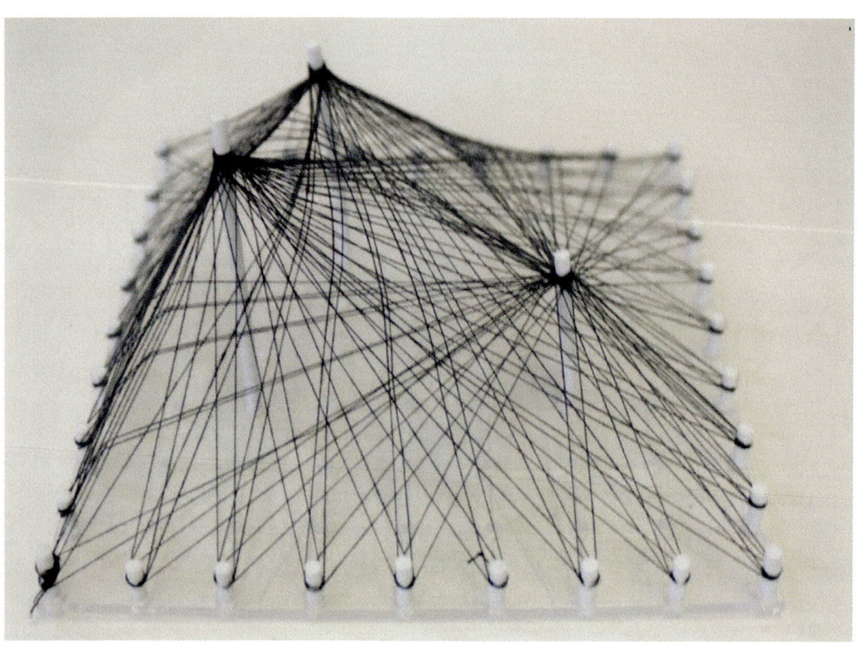

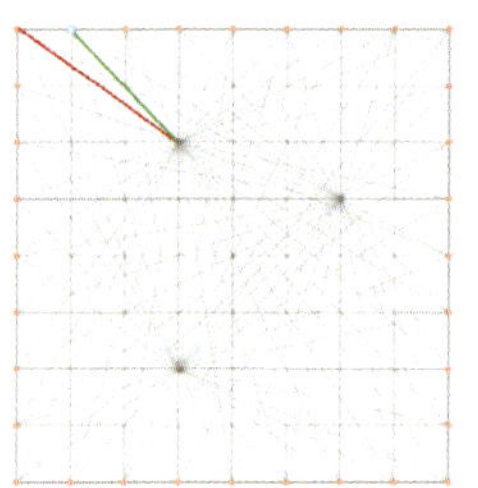

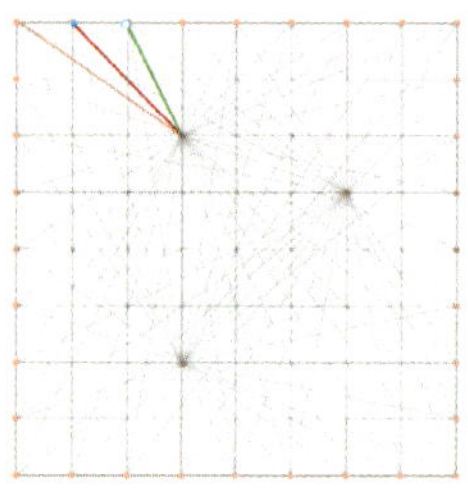

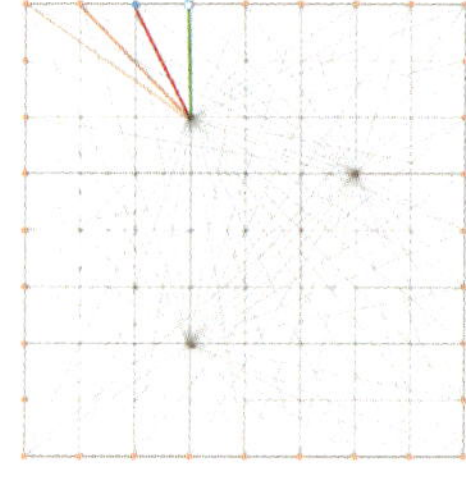

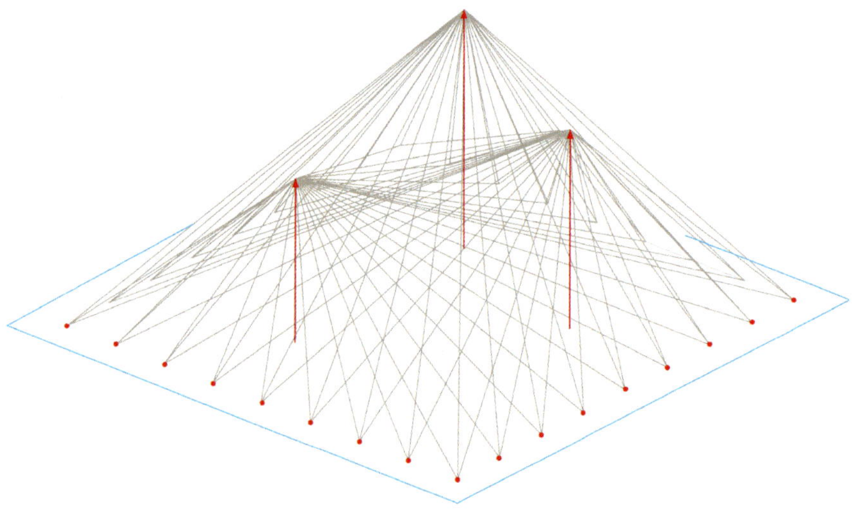

Above and following page: Three-dimensional models and studies of algorithmic explorations.

George Athanasopoulos, Brian Chu

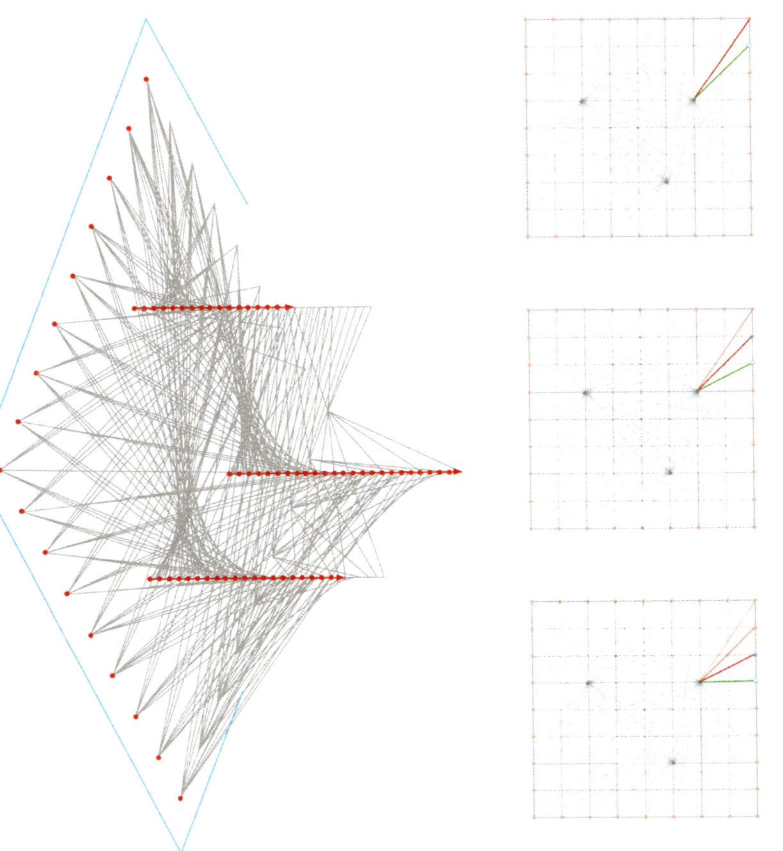

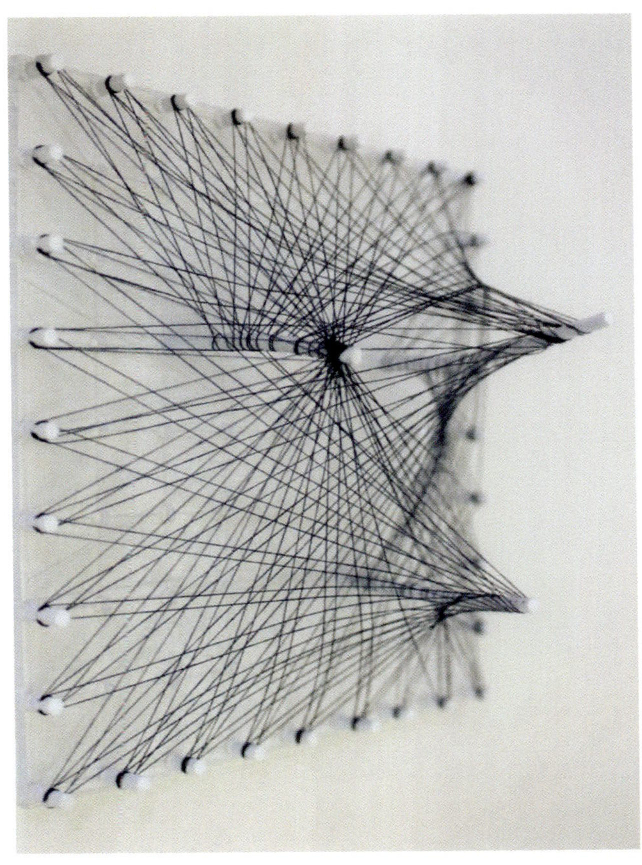

Three-dimensional winding model showing intersection and layered-embedded elements.

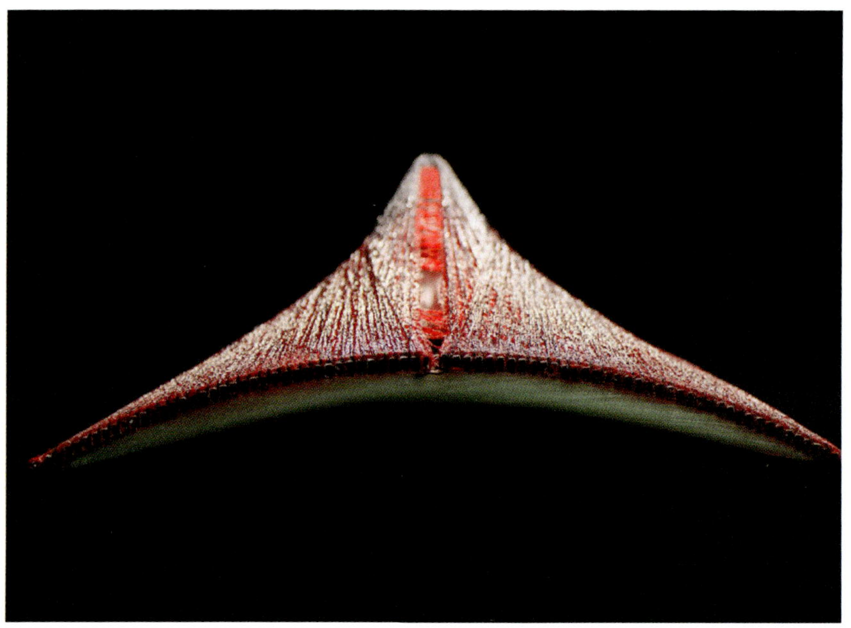

Above: Proto-architectural morphology axonometric and model.

Following page: Wrapping sequence of proto-architectural morphology.

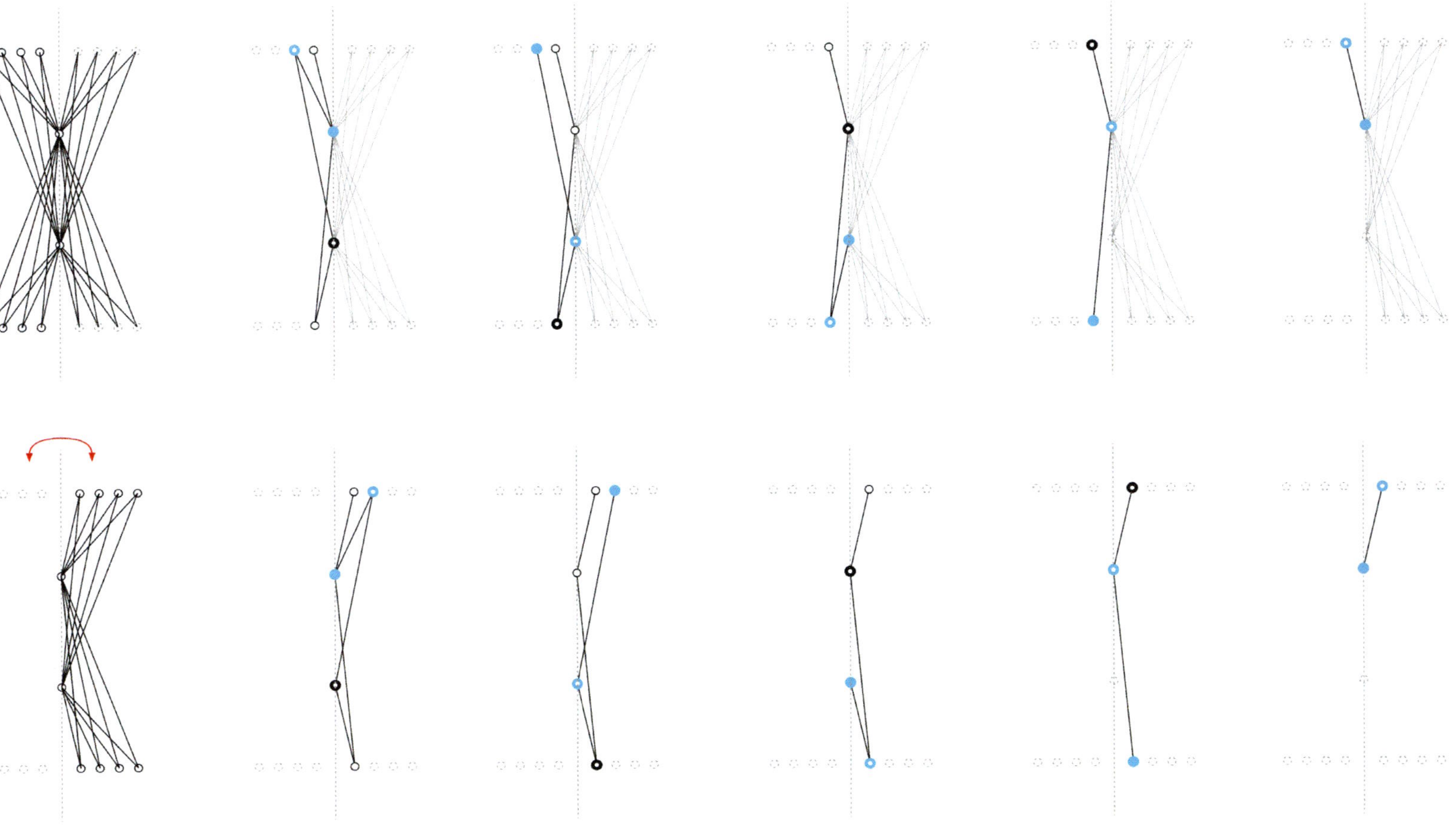

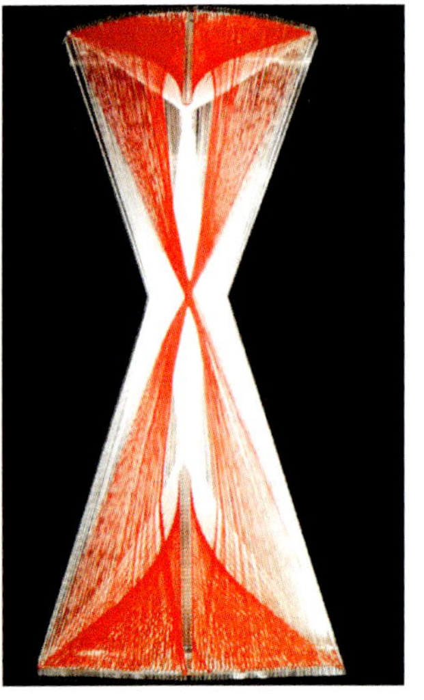

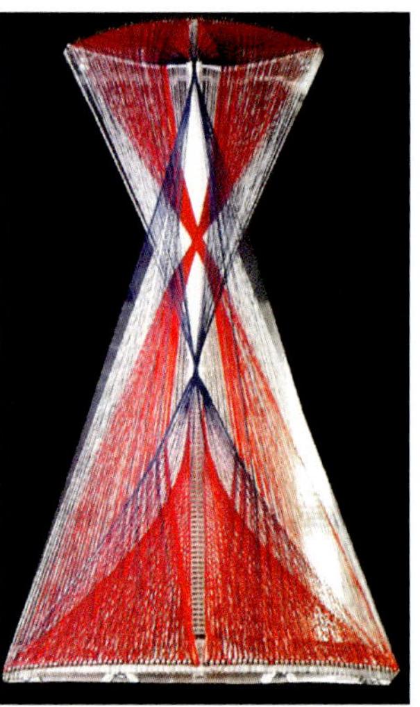

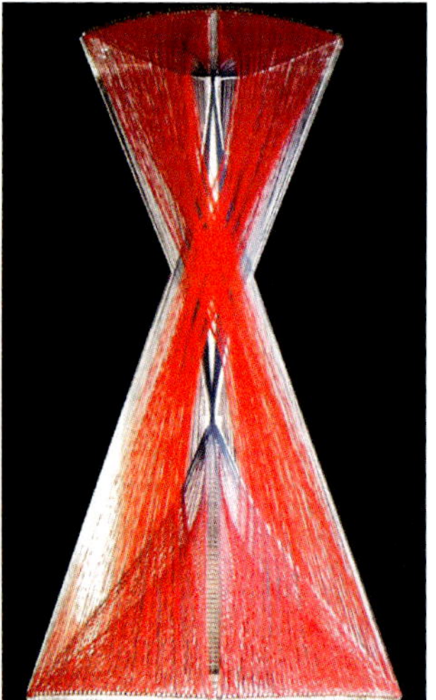

Top: Proto-architectural morphology model section.

Bottom: Layered hiearchical system of proto-architectural morphology.

Following page: Proto-architectural morphology model detail.

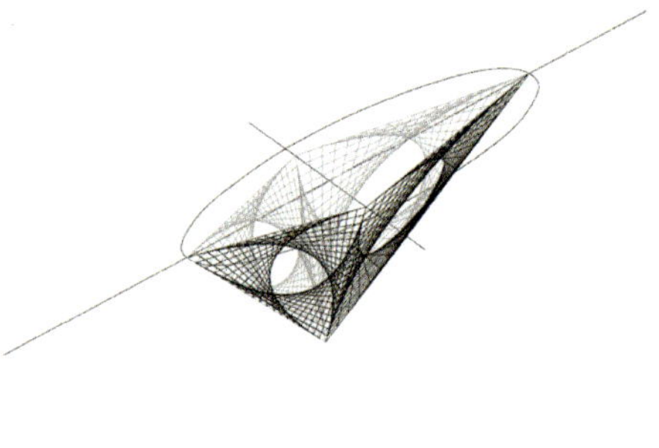

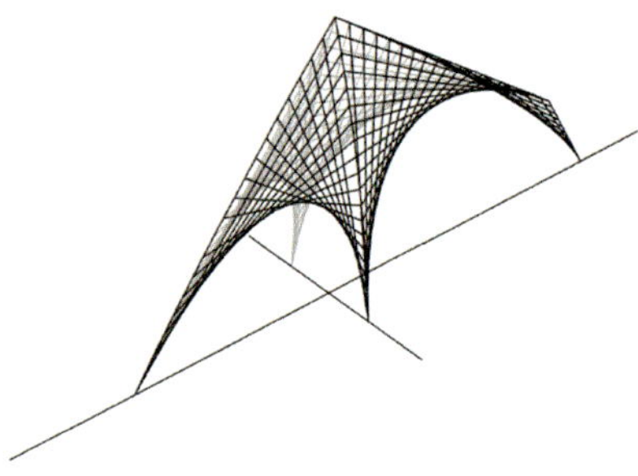

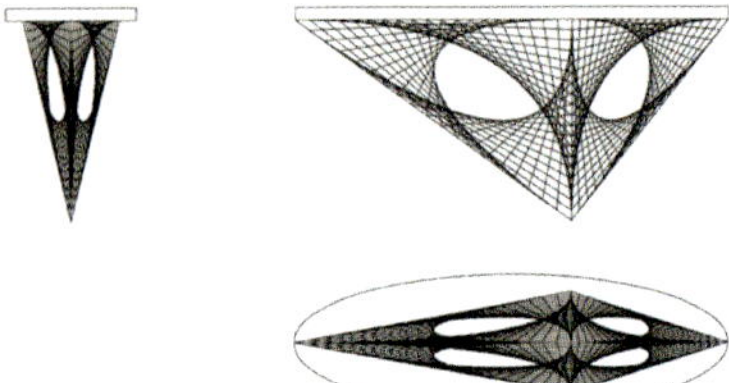

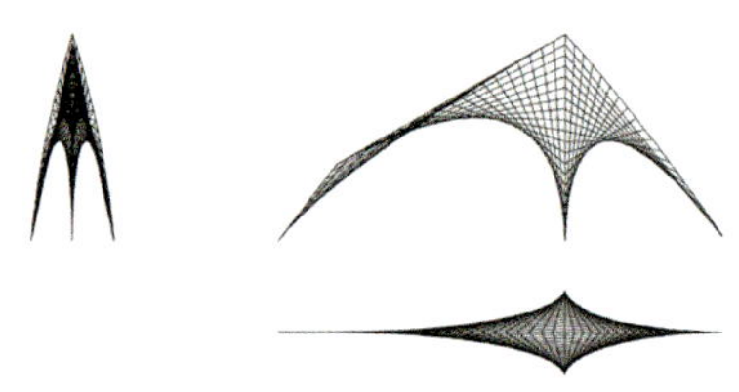

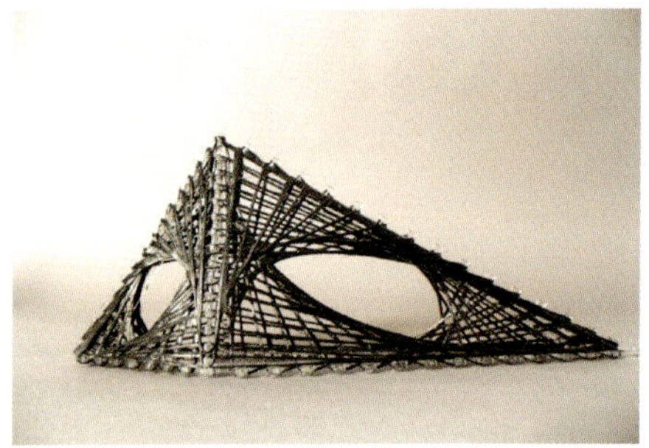

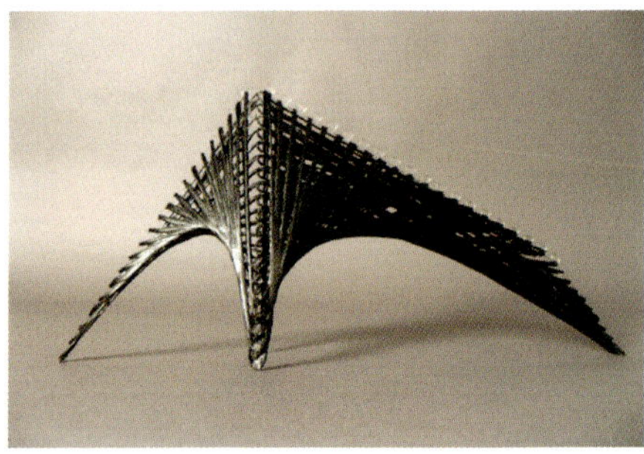

Top: Proto-architectural morphology proposals; drawings show wrapping logics.

Bottom: Proto-architectural morphology proposals in carbon-fiber models.

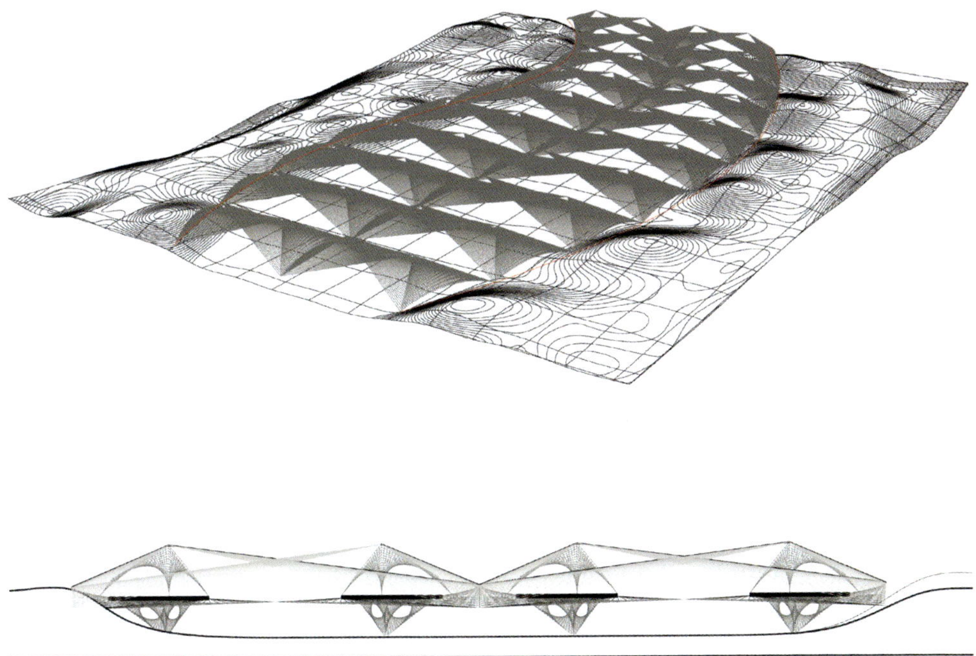

Top: Axonometric and sectional drawings of proposed architectural infrastructure based on wrapping logic.

Bottom: Perspective view of proposed architectural infrastructure model.

# Pneumatic Fibrous Form

Erin Cuevas
Mike Johnson
Jana Masset



Inspired by pneumatic-like structures found in nature, our project utilizes carbon-and-glass-fiber to translate biological constructs into architectural space. The system consists of two parts: first, a sectional cell structure; second, a pair of surfaces, consisting of a fibrous layer and a membrane layer which enclose the cell structure. These integrated design components rely on the inherent qualities of fibrous materials—providing both performative and experiential functions, while responding parametrically to desired structural, spatial, and luminous qualities. Our project ultimately exemplifies the seamless relationship between function and aesthetic, allowing quantitative material performance to be understood through diverse architectural experiences.

Efficient material performance is often exemplified in biological precedents. This project is rooted in the research of fibrous structures in organisms. In many natural systems, pneumatic-like elements and fibers work together to form complex structural networks. A "pneu" is a structure with an envelope and a filling, such as cells—membrane structures filled predominantly with water. Pneus form most soft-bodied organisms as well as rigid structures by shaping and orienting fibers. These pneumatically formed fibers serve as compression reinforcements, providing strength for organisms with rigid structural systems.

Bones serve as a primary example of a biological compression-reinforcement structure. Bones are formed by a cell called an osteoblast, which creates an extracellular matrix of hardened collagen-fibers; this network becomes a rigid structure, where pneumatically formed fibrous columns hold together the bone's surface. This structure operates at the local scale of each compression reinforcement, and also defines characteristics of the bone's overall form. We found this natural process particularly interesting, as the inflated fibrous material defines natural forms at both micro and macro scales.

We searched for functionally and morphologically similar examples in architecture, and arrived at double-membrane cushion structures. This typology keeps its global form simply by maintaining inflation between two membranes, connected by stringers of varying lengths.

Cushion structures have been deployed for a wide range of uses, from temporary construction tents to refined architectural projects, exemplified by Kengo Kuma's translucent inflated tea house in Frankfurt. Taking a more experimental cushion-structure approach, the firm Numen/For Use designs large pneumatic spaces with complex fibrous interiors, expanding highly interactive and experiential spaces upon inflation of an outer membrane.

While these projects illustrate the potential of pneumatics in architecture, they lack the ability to maintain their form without constant inflation. The precedents exemplify structures that are air-supported rather than formed through temporary air inflation. Carbon-and-glass-fiber serve as promising materials to explore pneumatically formed construction, given their light and strong traits when cured with a matrix such as epoxy resin. These materials, when implemented using principles of pneumaticity in bones, can generate static pneumatically formed fibrous architecture.

In order for cushion structures to adapt to qualities of rigid biological structural systems, carbon-and-glass-fibers must act in two ways: as compression reinforcements within a cellular wall section, as well as a structural double-membrane skin. For both of these systems, we developed specific numeric algorithms as a guide for the fibrous materials, allowing them to perform both structurally and experientially.

As opposed to traditional cushion-structure stringers that act in tension only while inflation is maintained between the membranes on either side, we were interested in identifying a fiber arrangement that could provide compression reinforcement as a composite system, taking advantage of the sectional depth of the assembly. In our research, we observed that an array of adjacent, round pneus will form polygonal shapes when placed under pressure from above and below, as the intersections between pneus form planar cell-walls. With this process in mind, we inflated pneus between two acrylic sheets to study how fiber stringers operate within a pressurized cell grid. We performed a series of algorithmic experiments, exploring how fibers of various lengths and organizations responded to this pneumatic interaction. We confirmed that fibers strung in tension between acrylic sheets adjust minimally to the pneumatic inflation, as expected; fibers with slack react more organically, shaping themselves to the pneus. We also noticed that slack strings bundle upon inflation, forming columns of multiple fibers. While utilizing a simple, rectangular array of pneus for overall control, we found that a diagonal bracing system offers the most robust support for containing pneumatic cells, while also yielding multiple points of structural fiber-to-fiber interaction. Carbon-fiber serves as the appropriate material for this diagonal matrix; it has high tensile strength and gains compressive strength upon hardening into a composite with resin. In addition to the diagonally oriented carbon-fibers, "vertical" stringers—fibers that attach to specific points on each surface of the double-membrane system—control the overall global form. These stringers are pulled in tension upon inflation, while maintaining the slack of the diagonal fibers to adjust naturally to the pneumatics. Because they take no structural load after all fibers are cured with a matrix, the vertical stringers could be constructed of any economic, inelastic fibrous material found in construction practices. These form-making vertical stringers, in conjunction with the diagonal fibers, form the sectional component of our system.

In addition to gaining control over the cell array, we conducted experiments to develop the double-membrane skin system. We focused on effects of varying fiber densities. Our goal was to form gradient transitions between opaque and transparent regions using controlled fiber patterns. To accomplish this, we first produced a formula, outputting an initial list of skip points along a perimeter which result in a homogeneous two-dimensional pattern when fibers are placed accordingly. A script then pulls a user input of desired transparency locations, and reroutes fibers that pass through these regions. The script parametrically relocates fiber paths, allowing control over the size, quantity, and shape of transparent regions, as well as the transitional depth between sparse and dense fibers. This process is malleable to many forms, and sustains varying fiber density as desired.

The aforementioned algorithm serves as a crucial tool in the formation of the membrane system. We initially studied the carbon-fiber algorithm as a single-layered skin to contain the pneumatic cell array, but we determined an additional material was necessary for weatherproofing. As a second membrane layer, translucent and transparent materials best maintained an airtight system while simultaneously transmitting light and shadow. We used thermoplastic inflation to mimic the spatial effects that would be achieved by other, more available translucent materials found in architectural construction. From these experiments, we resolved that fully transparent materials generate the most successful luminous qualities, especially within the double-membrane section. The carbon-fiber-strung skin, together with the transparent surface, form a composite that defines our membrane system.

With the layered surface components resolved, we were equipped to bring all our experiments into a single, cohesive system. To be clear, our complete system is composed of four distinct elements: (1) On each exterior face—a carbon-fiber surface, placed using an algorithm controlling density, (2) layered within each carbon-fiber surface—an interior transparent membrane, to maintain an airtight system, and to reinforce the carbon-fiber surface structure, (3) between the membranes—diagonally-oriented carbon-fiber matrix, to provide structural and inhabitable depth to the system, and (4) between the surfaces—non-structural stringers, controlling the overall global form. The first and second elements form the membrane component of the system, and the third and fourth form the sectional component.

When employing this system at an architectural scale, any desired form must be divided into developable segments for ease of construction, because the stringers operate most precisely on a single-curved surface. As a construction process, the four system elements are integrated into each divided segment, then inflated with pneus and resined. Pneus are then removed upon hardening, and each segment is joined together. The result encompasses inhabitable exterior surfaces, as well as interior spaces within the depth of the cell section.

To test this system, we designed a proto-architectural morphology: a form used to demonstrate the multifaceted qualities inherent to the system. By using an overall form, generated from lofted closed splines, we are able to showcase the system's potential to operate as surfaces in multiple orientations. As these sections vary in shape, the loft expands and contracts, opening spaces for human interaction inside and outside the structure. Rather than applying the cellular grid in an orthogonal rectangular array, as we did in tests, we shifted points to create a diagrid: this prevents structural faults at critical locations along the lofted form, and also helps to resist shear force. Linear attractors manipulate the diagrid, to concentrate the cells into dense regions at structurally weak locations and to widen them at locations of inhabitable space. The applied fibrous surface algorithm allocates varied moments of transparency and opacity on the interior and exterior, while simultaneously providing support for floor surfaces.

The resulting morphology exhibits the system's adaptability as structure, skin, and inhabitable space—all within a single form. While we are able to design isolated moments of the morphology, the amalgamation of our performative components produces many unexpected architectural episodes, bringing life to the form. The system's layered and transparent nature allows primarily functional elements, such as the varying depth of the stringers and diagonal matrix, to be understood through spatial moments. In this way, the project challenges the relationship between performance and experience; our morphology brings these two distinct qualities together, providing a platform for them to operate harmoniously.

Following page: Matrix of diagrams and fiber structures of project components.

I: SECTION

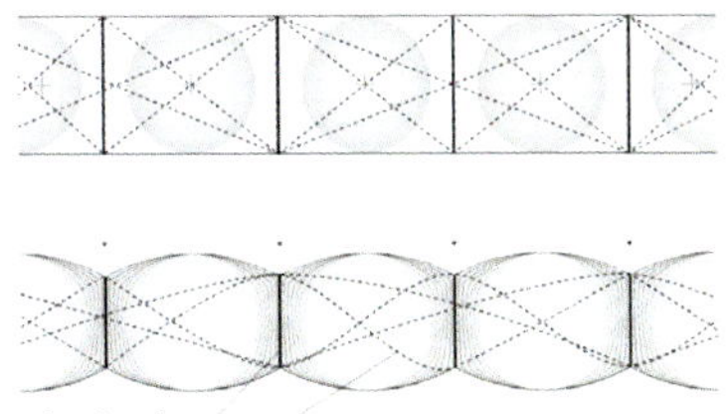

structural
diagonal
stringers provide
form and cell
organization

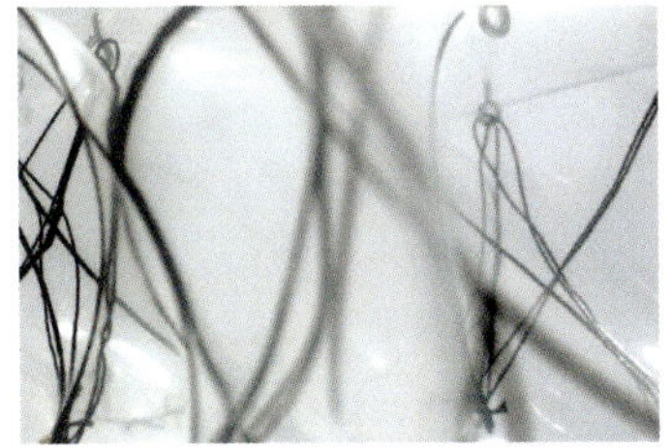

2: SURFACE + MEMBRANE

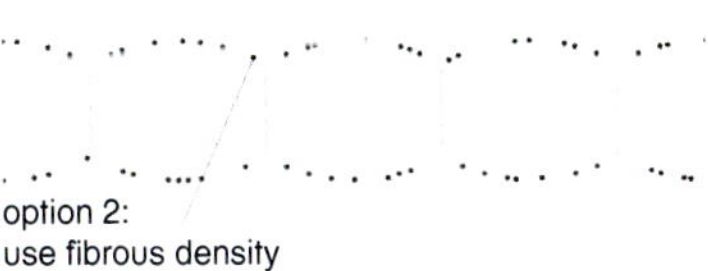

option 2:
use fibrous density
algorithm as membrane

3: SYSTEM + CONSTRUCTION

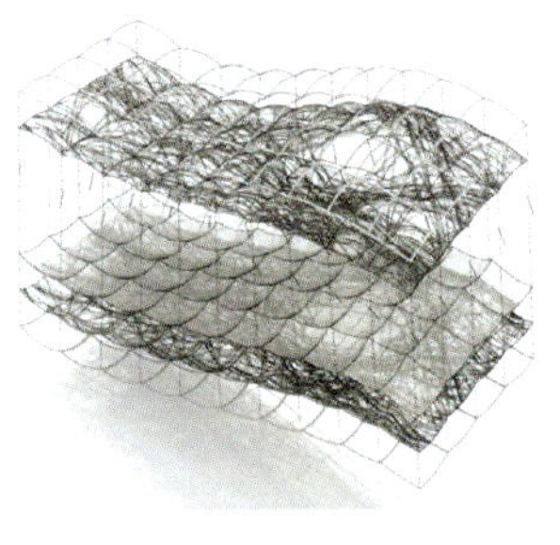

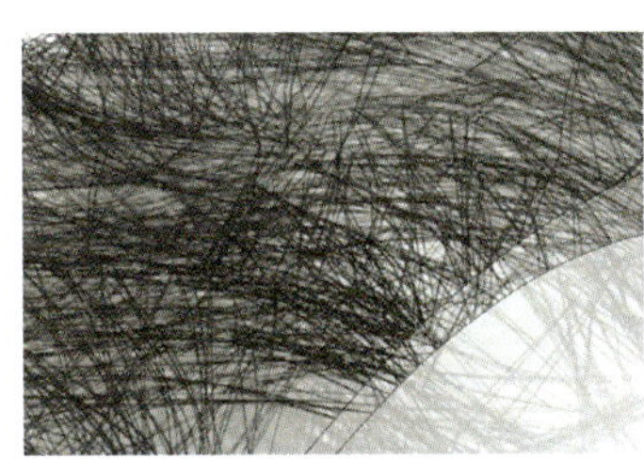

3: SYSTEM + CONSTRUCTION

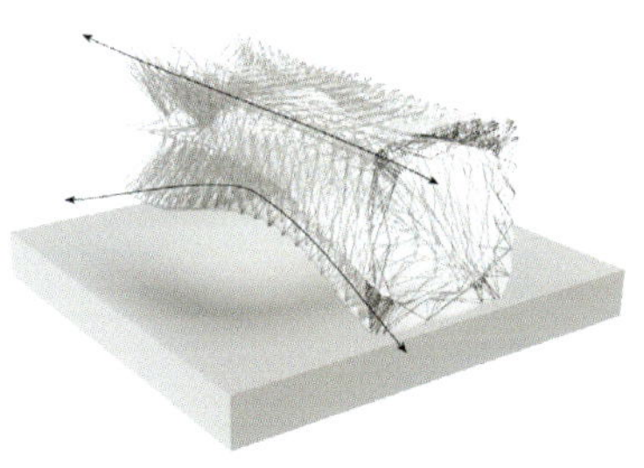

Pneumatic Fibrous Form

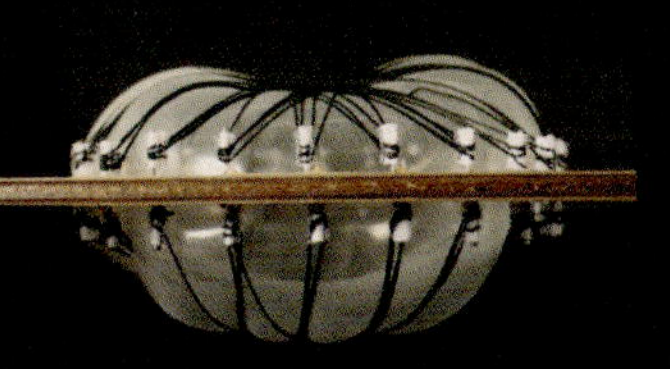

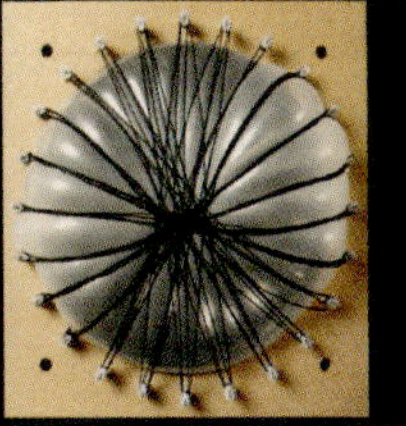

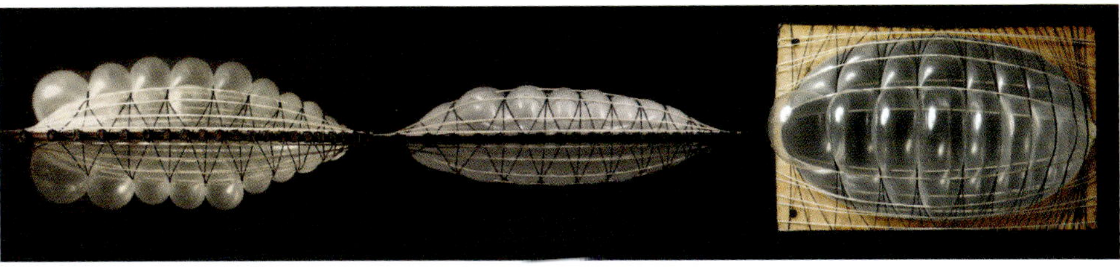

Previous page: Top view of slack bundling model with pneu separation.

Top: Variations in bundling with slack and pneu separation using multiple strings versus a single string.

Bottom: Slack-bundling model, detail, with multi-string separation.

CELL
WALLS

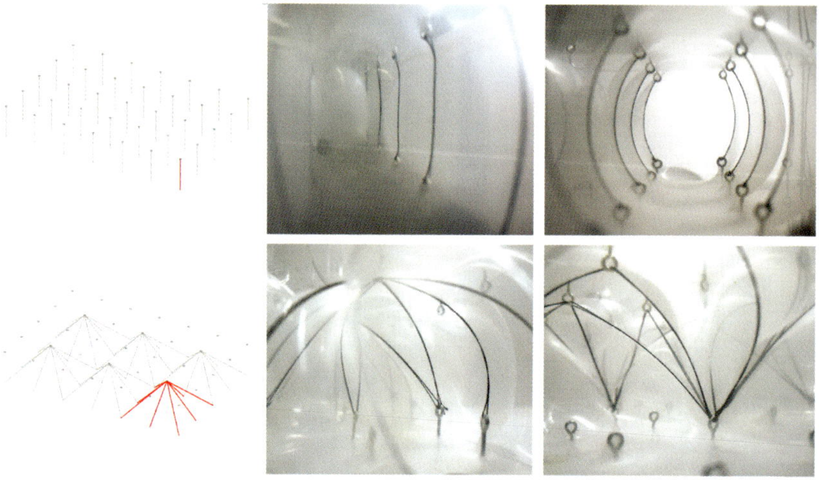

DOUBLE-
LAYERED

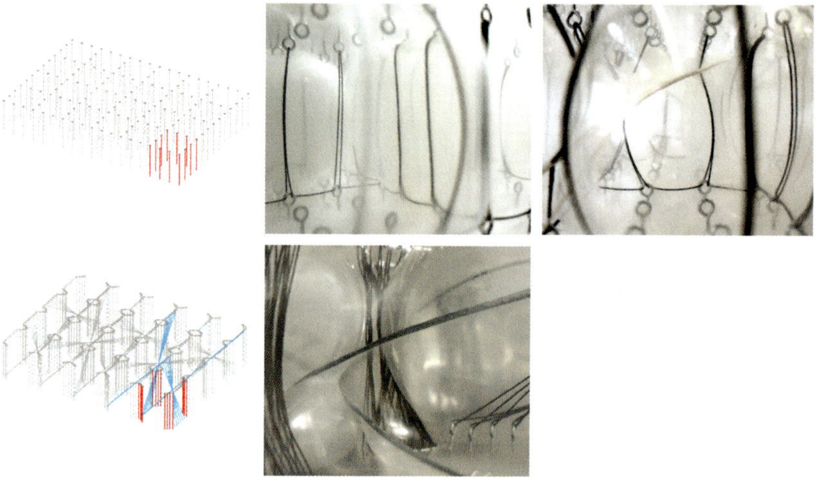

DIAGONAL
BRACING

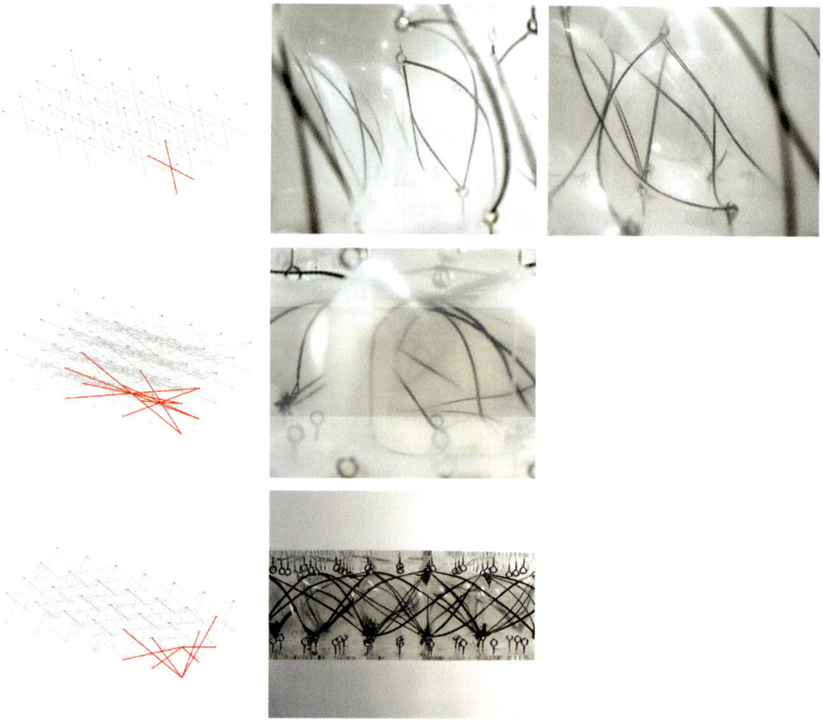

Previous page: Sections showing pneumatic interaction forms.

Above: Physical model showing pneumatic form.

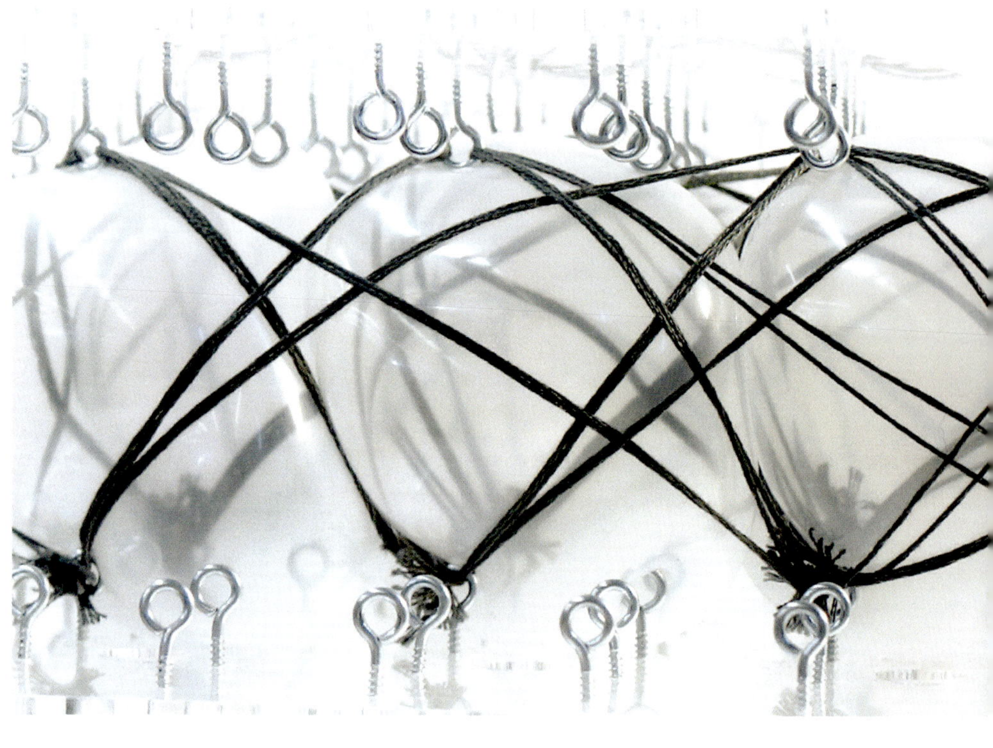

Top: Experimental model of diagonal bracing with one skip providing strong cell-wall support.

Bottom: Experimental model of linear-fiber formation as a result of a single pneu inflation.

Following page: Linear-fiber formation, model detail, as a result of a single pneu inflation.

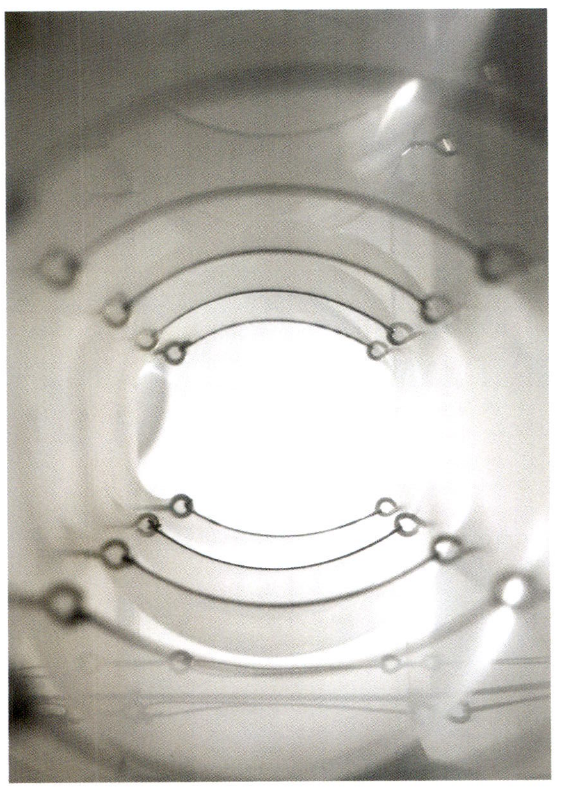

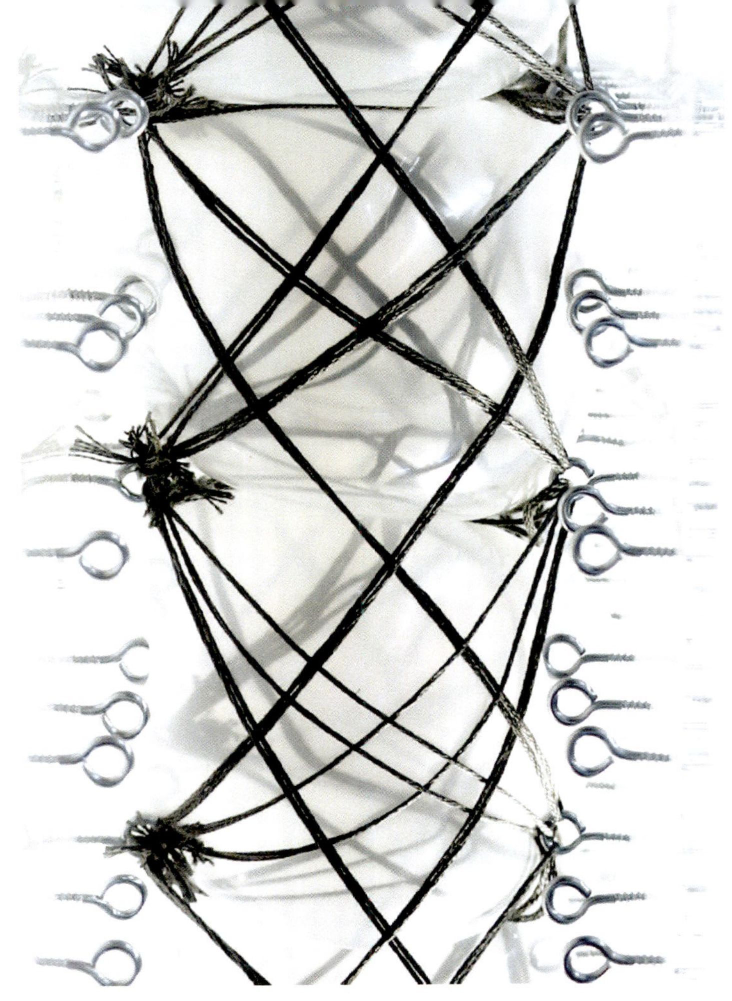

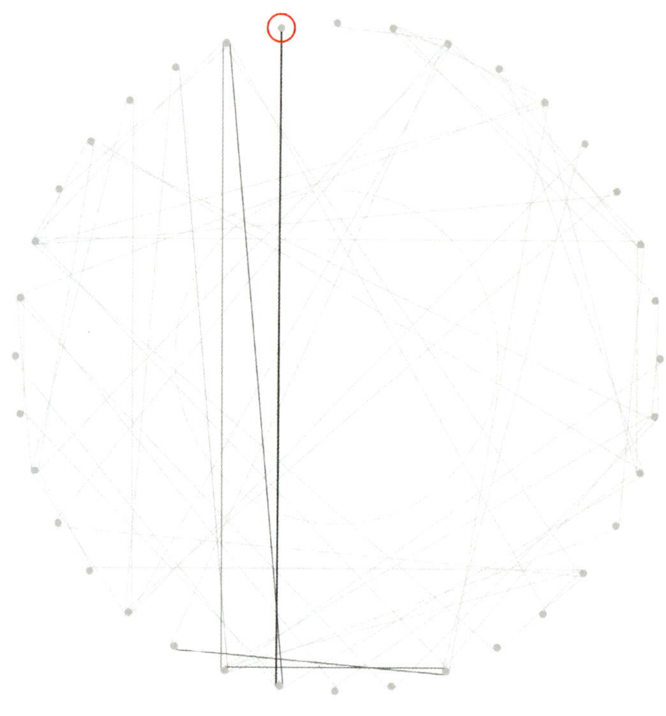

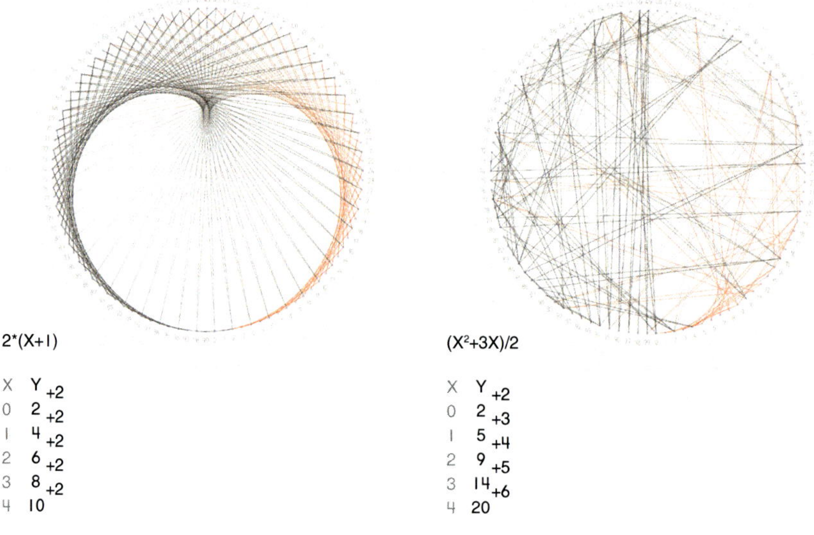


Top: Diagram of fiber-placement logic.

Bottom: Algorithmic articulation of fiber-winding patterns.

Following page: Two-dimensional gradient studies of fiber placement.

LINEAR GRADIENT

LINEAR GRADIENT

RADIAL GRADIENT

RADIAL GRADIENT

RADIAL GRADIENT

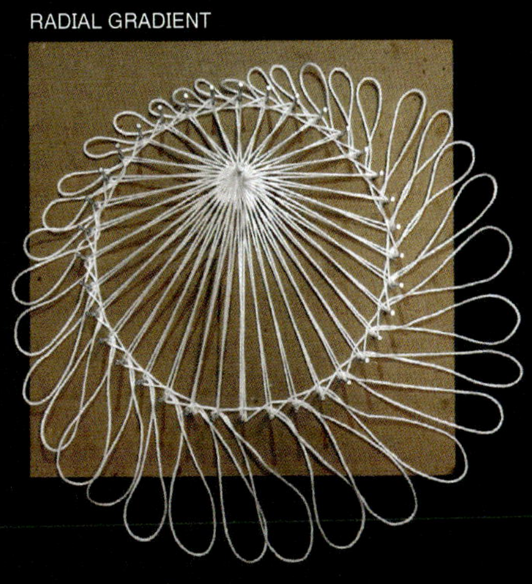

RADIAL ALGORITHM

Above: Series of models showing density with linear algorithm applied to pneumatic layers in exploring visual transparency and reflection.

Following page: Exploratory model with visual transparency and reflection.

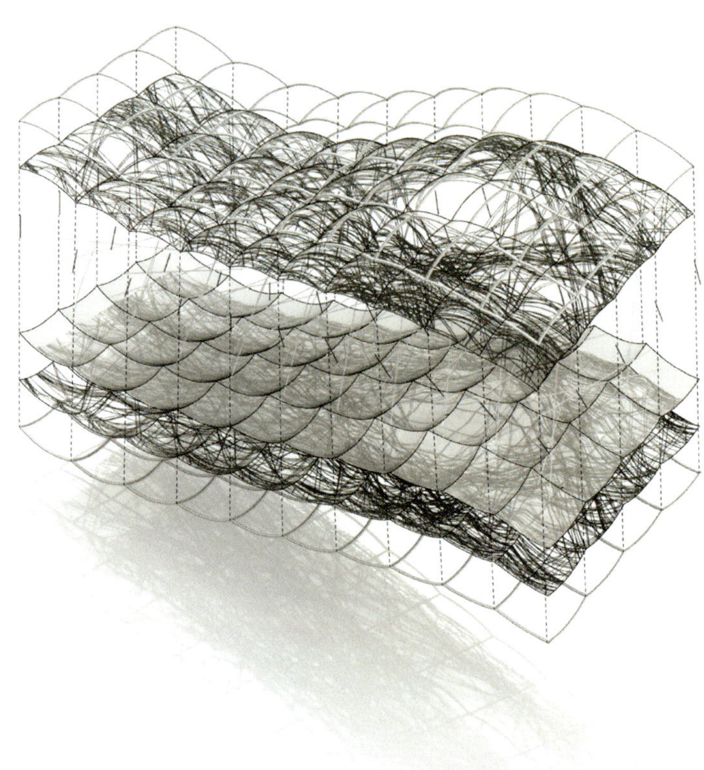


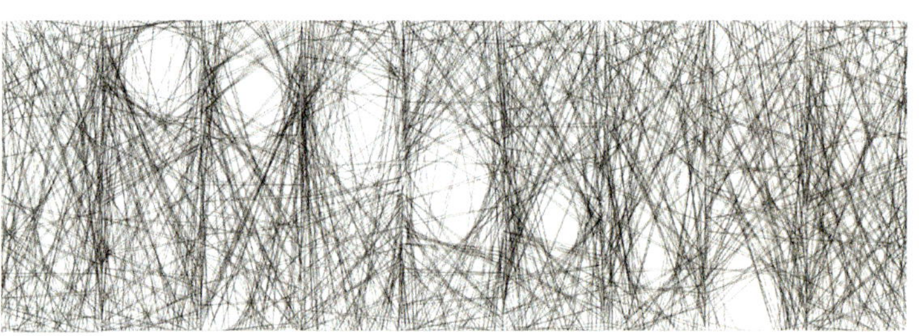

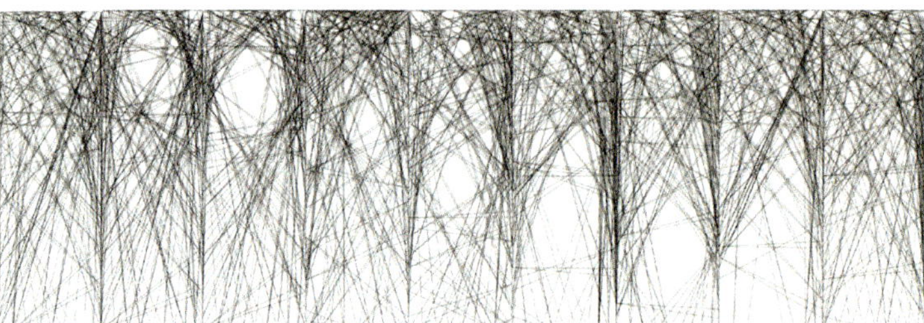

Top: Layered axometric of pneumatic form.

Bottom: Diagram of patched algorithm with equally spaced points versus point gradients.

Following page: Model showing formation of density algorithm and translucent membrane with soft shadows.

Top: Layered axonometric of light quality of proto-architectural morphology.

Bottom: Proto-architectural morphology diagrams showing diagrid formal resolution, algorithm exterior surface, and diagonal bracing density.

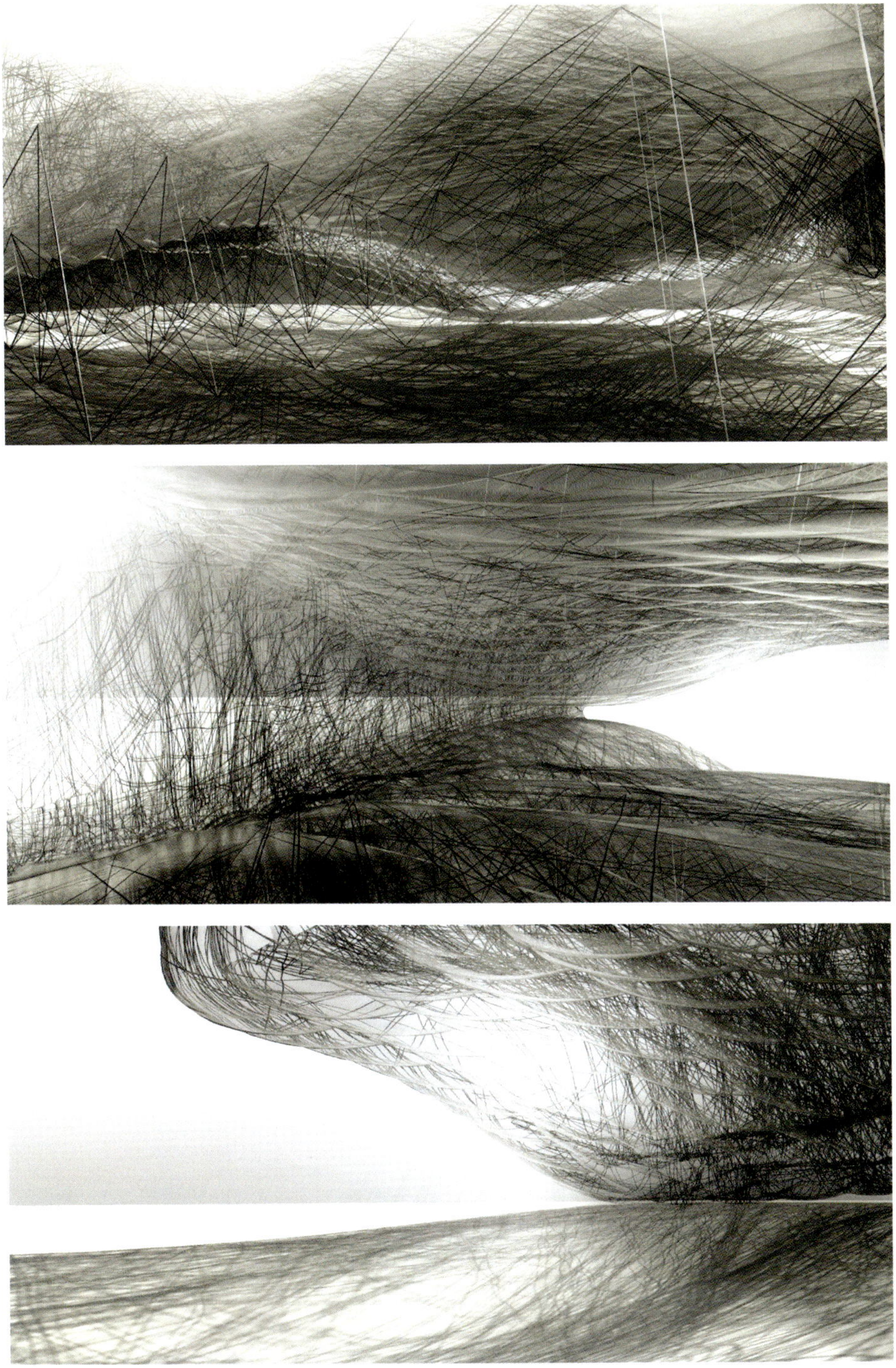

Renderings of proto-architectural morphology.

# Form-Active Fibrous-Composite Structural Surface

Wenling Li
Christopher Meyer
Chase Pitner



The studio Material Performance: Composite Morphology and Fibrous Tectonics afforded the opportunity to conduct rigorous research and investigation into existing and emerging methods of fibrous-composite material systems within architecture. Our investigations focused on developing a critical understanding of the material characteristics embedded within the carbon-and-glass-fiber-composites. Research revealed that fibrous composite systems were introduced within architectural applications in the early 1950-60s exemplified by the collaboration between Monsanto Chemical Company and MIT in the design and construction of the Monsanto House. The Monsanto House captured the innovative potential of this material-systems ability to articulate more complex geometries while tectonically yielding a high structure-to-weight ratio. Fibrous composites emerged as a leading innovation in architectural tectonic and material systems in the 1950-60s, yet has not deviated from original form-based application processes in current use today. This is evident in the construction of the SFMOMA expansion, which will represent the largest use of fibrous-composite construction in the United States once completed in 2016.

Fibrous-composite applications in architecture have relied heavily on the material-systems ability to achieve more complex geometries, evident in the 1960s Futura House and Zaha Hadid's Chanel Pavilion. Our research is focused on developing a critical understanding of new applications or processes of fibrous-composite system in architecture. Utilizing carbon-and-glass-fiber composites as a medium in which to test the integration of form, structure, and resulting material properties. Initial investigations employed the use of cotton fiber as this system provided a scalar representation of carbon-and-glass-fiber. However, early research revealed an increased elasticity in cotton-fiber systems as compared to carbon- or glass-fiber.

Depth-active structural systems (i.e. metal I-beam extrusions), in this case single-section profile extrusions, are used as full-length structural members. The aggregate loads a structural member will carry determine the size and shape of the extrusion section. Fundamental to depth-active structural systems is the understandings that, the increase in loads is counteracted by the increase in structural depth through added material. Inherent to the nature of extrusions, portions of the structural member are not necessary to carry load but are instead a residual condition of the extrusion process.

Heinrich Engle defined "Form-Active Structural systems as a system, which transmits loads only through simple normal stresses, either through tension or compression, without bending." Engle outlines predecessors of Form-Active Structures which included Catenary, Funicular Arch, Tensile Membrane, and Compression-only Shells. In current architectural practice the design of form and structure have been separated into two separate processes, as the architect designs the form, then an engineer rationalizes the form through the configuration of material.

Fibrous-composite form-active structural systems challenge the current paradigm, as this system has the potential to incorporate the design of material, form, and structure into the thickness of a single surface. Fibrous-composite systems can produce heterogeneous surface conditions as the algorithm and scaffold have the potential to produce various structural conditions, translucencies, and apertures within a single surface. No other material system is able to achieve similar capacities within a single surface.

Our investigations focused on the application process of free-formed fibrous-composite systems that are composed of continuous carbon-and-glass-fiber rovings. This process varies from traditional mold-based applications that compress layers of chopped-fiber mats resulting in continuous fiber-to-fiber interaction throughout the surface. Free-formed fibrous-composite applications utilize a temporary scaffolding mechanism, which provide limited points of support or contact in the application process. This allows the fibers to act freely in varying conditions of tension or compression throughout the surface.

Initial investigation focused on fundamental algorithmic studies through basic line drawings, computer modeling, parametric analysis, and physical models. The necessary descriptions of the terms Algorithm and Scaffolding specific to the studio Material Performance: Composite Morphology and Fibrous Tectonics are as followed.

Algorithm: a process or set of rules to be followed in calculations or other problem solving operations, especially by a computer. The definition of the term algorithm in the context of the studio Material Performance, will refer to the deployment of glass-and-carbon-fiber through a specific arrangement.

Scaffolding: a temporary structure on the outside of a building made usually of wooden planks and metal poles. The definition of the term scaffolding in the context of the studio Material Performance will refer to a temporary structure in which glass-and-carbon-fiber are laid through a fiber-laminate process to be hardened with resin. The hardened fibrous system becomes a surface, which is separated from the temporary scaffolding structure. Scaffoldings used are generally constructed from materials ranging from chipboard, plexi or acrylic, MDF, plywood and metal.

Our research began from the basic achievement of a complete fiber acting on fiber surface, which sets forth the premise of a structurally sound fiber-composite system. Using a baseline litmus of complete fiber-to-fiber engagement within a single surface, a systematic series of explorations were carried out using a range of scaffolding sets. The types of scaffoldings implemented can be categorized into parallel, mirrored, radial, multidirectional-open, and multidirectional-closed. Related to various scaffold conditions or sets, the variables of curvature both in plan and in section of the scaffoldings, various algorithmic deployment and fiber-laminate processes were adopted to guarantee continuity of full fiber-to-fiber interaction. The algorithmic deployment of fibers onto scaffolding explored in the initial investigations are listed as follows: 1) Single algorithm—The initial algorithmic study focused on basic fiber-to-fiber interaction, investigating a range of fiber placements that offer opportunities of fiber overlap. Physical models were generated using white cotton fiber string ultimately becoming a base layer of fiber. With the transition of the models into glass-and-carbon-fiber the base layer would be generated with glass-fiber and act as a secondary scaffolding for the carbon-fiber to engage. 2) Two part algorithm—The two part algorithm studies implemented a combination of algorithms to force fiber acting on fiber within the single surface. The study paired a base-layer fiber system with an addition layer of fiber to deflect the fibrous surface into a doubly curved system. The base-layer is generally comprised of white cotton fiber-or-glass-fiber while the second layer is composed of black cotton fiber or carbon-fiber. 3) Layered algorithm—The investigation into a layered algorithm exploits the deployment of multiple algorithms across specific surface conditions to maintain a complete lamination between fibers. Controlling the algorithmic fiber placement allows laminate of the individual fibrous layers to deflect the surface into form-active structural surface. 4) Selective wrap path—The use of single, two-part and layered algorithmic fiber-laminate acknowledges control of surface density and the deflection of fibrous layers into a form-active structural surface. The deployment of selective wrap paths unites the language of the structural surface, inclusive of single, two part, and layered algorithms, with aperture, edge termination, connections to bearing, bifurcation of form, bisecting surfaces, and Möbius formations.

The research stemming from the investigations of algorithm, fiber-laminate hierarchy, and scaffolding configuration developed into the early thoughts of an architectural morphology. The investigation pressured one question, where does the essence of a fiber-composite architecture exist. In the final phase of the project the research aimed to increase the complexity of architectural morphology and spatial conditions. The opportunities rooted in the fibrous-composites systems led to the achievement of embedded aperture within the surface, bisecting surfaces, bifurcating forms, and various connections to foundation conditions. The final architectural morphology realized five architectural conditions: foot condition, arching forms, Möbius Strip, aperture, and bifurcation while maintaining full fiber-to-fiber interaction within the surface and coherence between material, form and structure. The final carbon-and-glass-fiber integrated model realized a heterogeneous surface implying the ability to host programmatic entities such as transits stations.

In conclusion, the inquiry into the character of a fibrous-composite architecture engages the largely untapped potential of an architecture informed by the integration of designed material and form-active surface. Systematically questioning the relationship between material, form, and structure through research as part of the Material Performance: Composite Morphology and Fibrous Tectonics studio uncovered a systemic misunderstanding of the affiliations of structure, material, and form in the field of design. The open communication rooted in an informed logic between material, form, and structure offers new architectural possibilities uninhibited from the constraints of borrowed methodology.

Top: Form-active structural model showing hieararchical conditions of fiber-to-fiber interaction.

Bottom: Study model with varied positive and negative curvature along scaffolding.

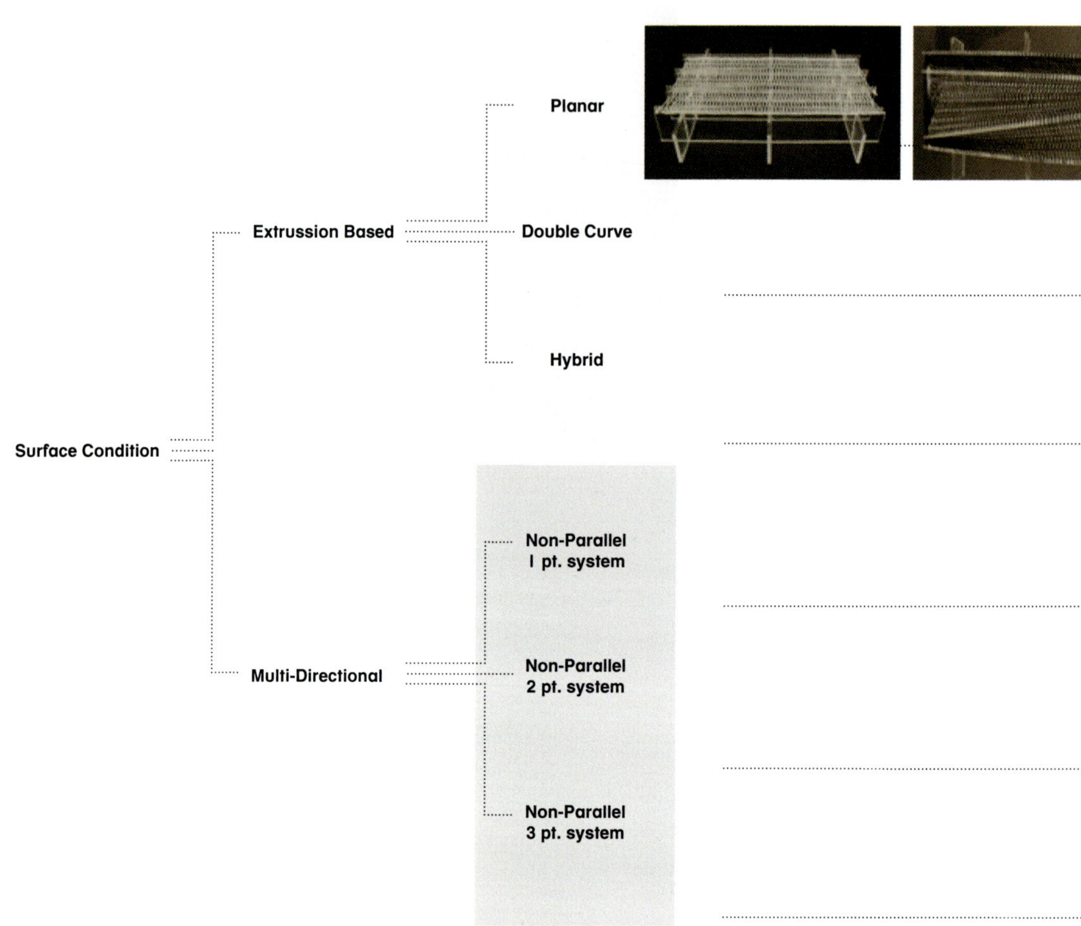


Phase 2 matrix diagramming the process of multi-directional systems.

**Process**

| Two Part Algorithm | Layered Algorithm | Optimal Algorithm Placement |
| --- | --- | --- |
| ase Algorithm – White Fiber)<br>ctive Algorithm – Black Fiber)<br>ased tension and compression | Apply 1/2 Base Algorithm<br>Deploy Active Algorithm<br>Apply other 1/2 Base Algorithm | Algorithm deployed within various areas of concavity and convexity to maintain fiber-to-fiber interaction |

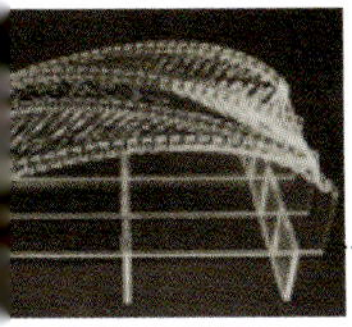

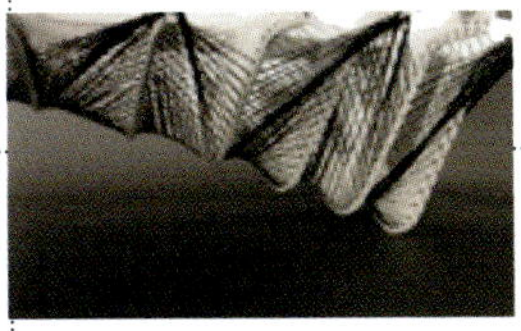

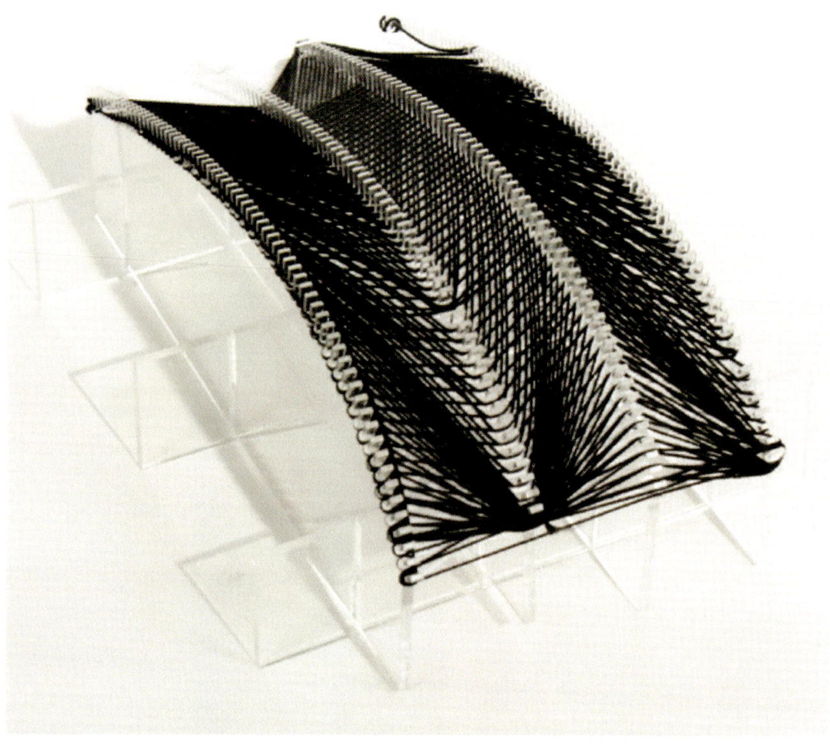

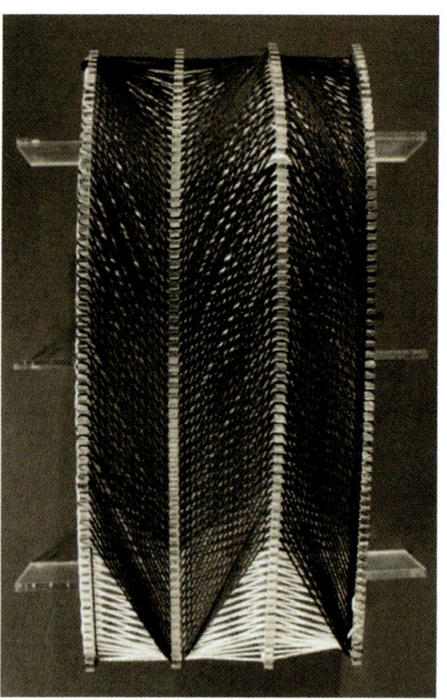

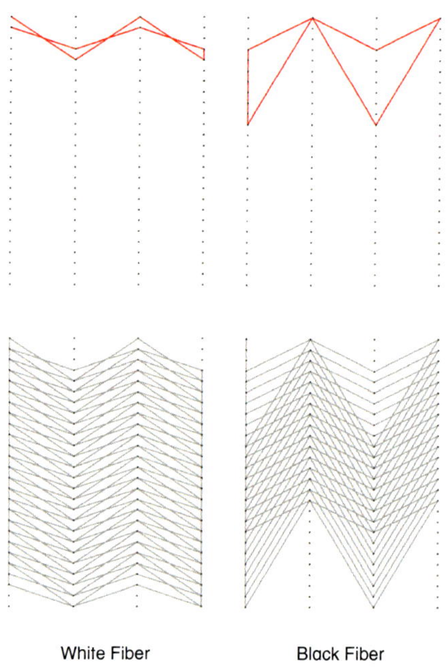


Above: Cotton-fiber prototype 3 details with parallel scaffolding and curved profile.

Above: Prototype 9 with parallel scaffold, convex-to-planar curves, and layered algorithm.

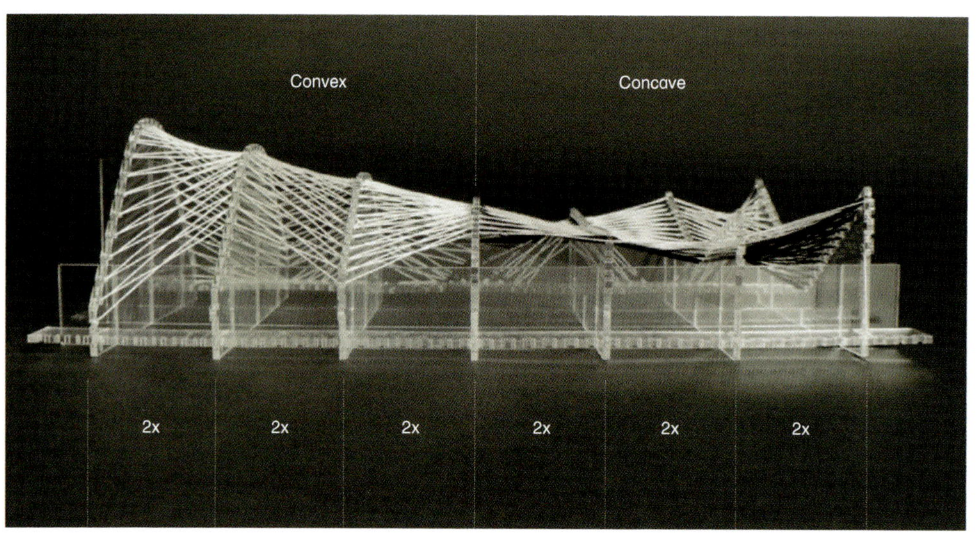


Top: Prototype 8 model with parallel scaffold, double-curved surface, and layered algorithm.

Bottom: Diagram of prototype 8 compontents.

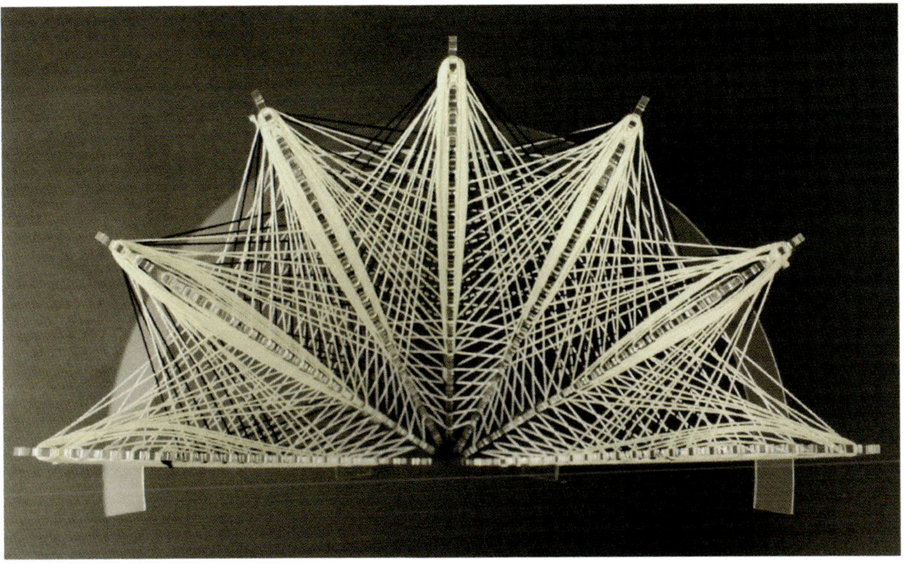

Model images of point radial system with parallel, covex, and concave-curve profiles.

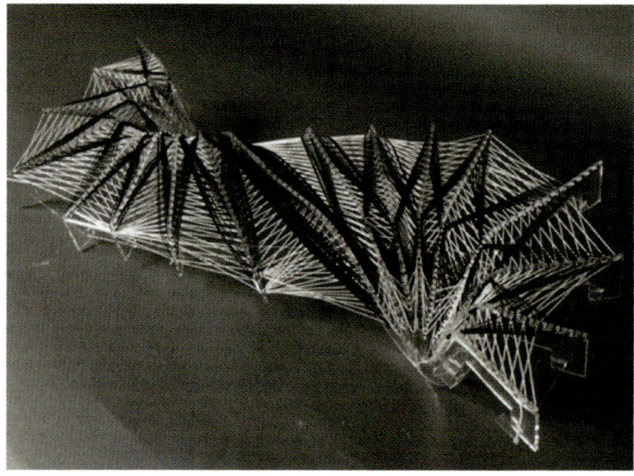

Above: Radial models of base algorithm (top), structural algorithm (middle), and tertiery wrap path (bottom).

Following page: 2-point-parallel radial system with convex, concave, and planar-curves.

Above: Scalar model showing positive and negative curvature in scaffolding ribs.

Following page: 2-point-mirrored radial system with postitive and negative curves increasing the form-active structural surface.

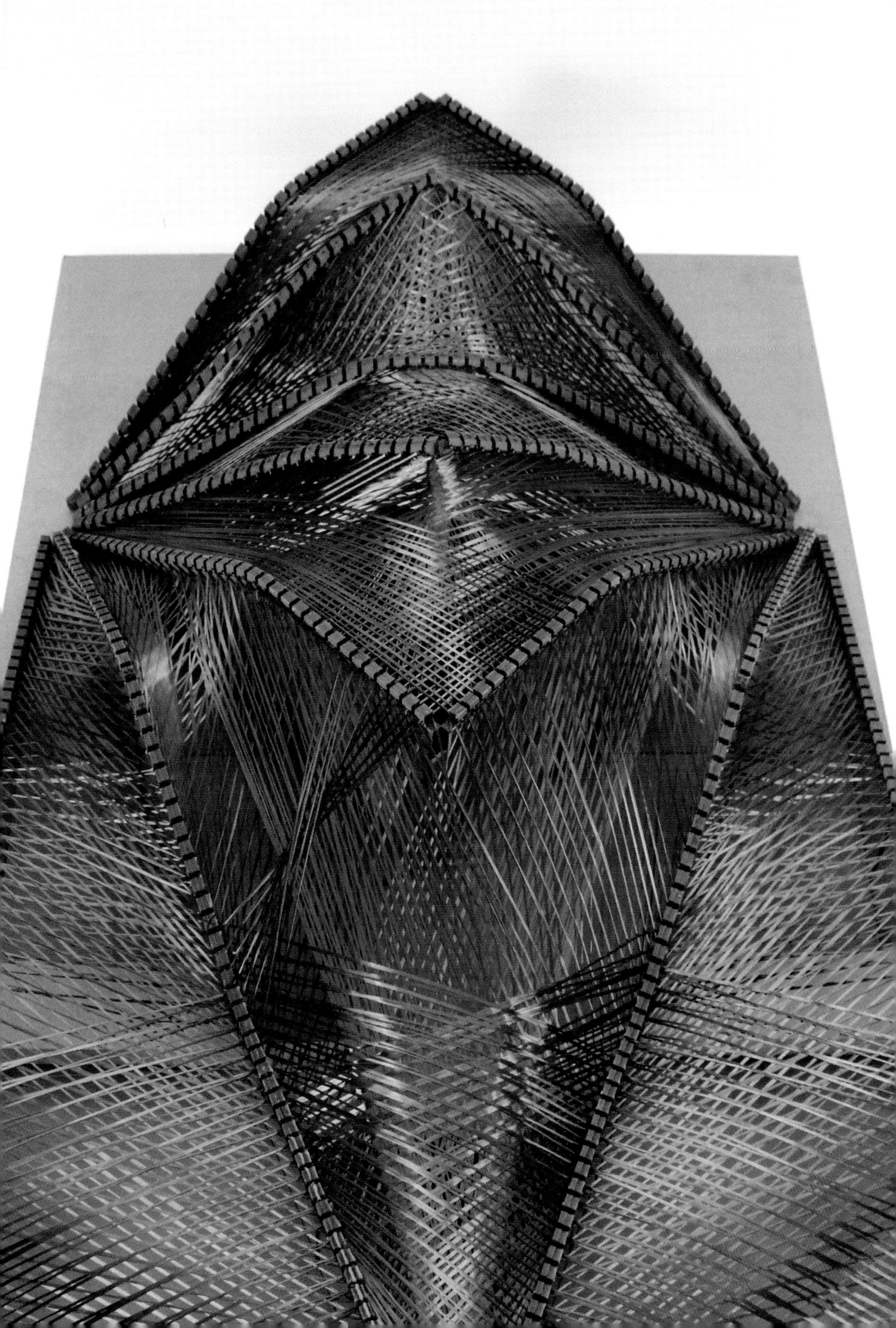

Top: Carbon-fiber model with increased fiber-to-fiber interaction showing spanning surface, foot condition, and edge condition.

Bottom: Form-active fibrous-composite structural surface showing emerging architectural elements.

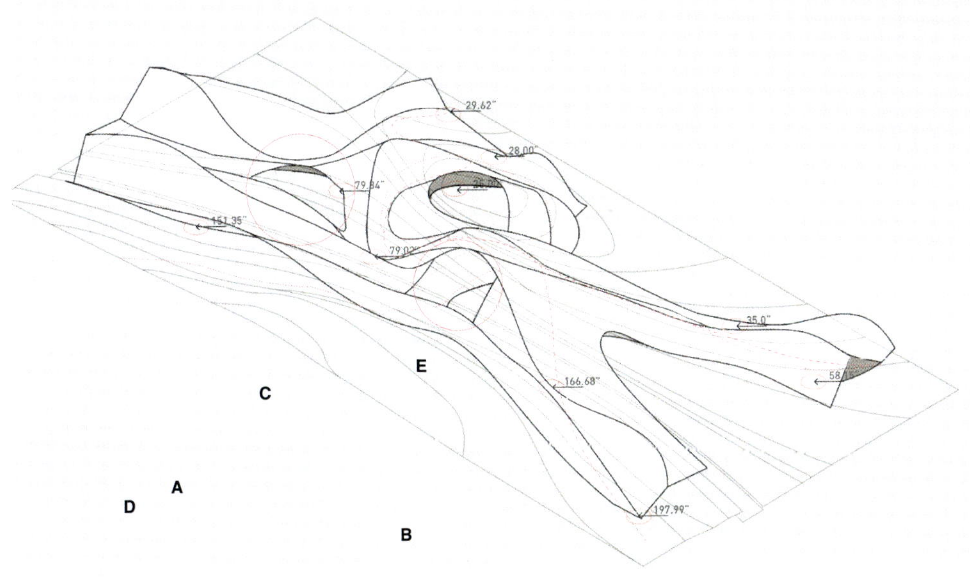






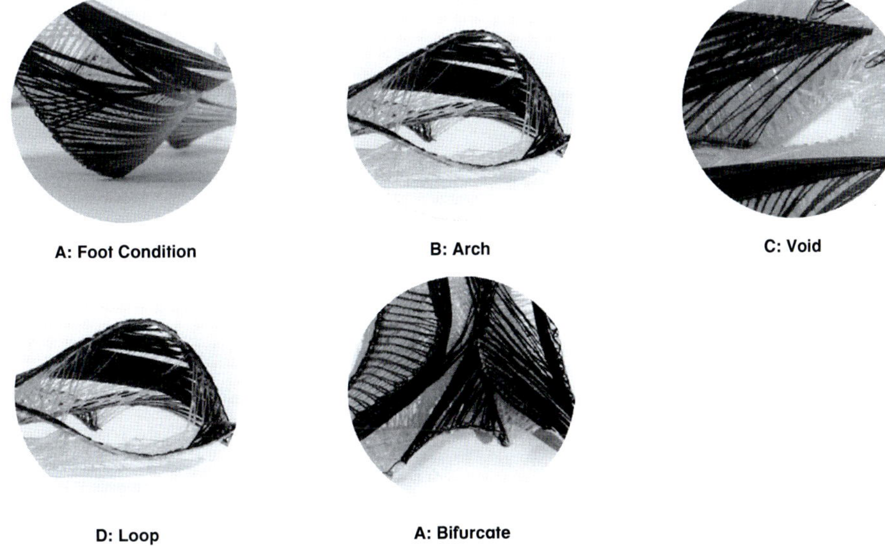


Above: Diagram of form-active fibrous-composite structural surface illustrating architectural conditions within system.

Following spread: 2-Point-mirrored radial system with postitive and negative curved scaffording increasing the form-active structural surface.

# Studies in Fiber Interaction

Iman Fayyad
Joshua Feldman



This project, Studies in Fiber Interaction, re-interprets the tectonic expression of doubly ruled surfaces. Such surfaces have long been the subject of structural and geometric interest among architectural engineers such as Felix Candela and Pier Luigi Nervi. The construction of these specific classes of anticlastic shell structures has played an important role in the evolution of building construction not only because of the structural capacities of the surface type, but also for the virtues of the straight ruling lines which are able to generate formwork and structure from conventional building materials. In most cases, however, the complex and visually intricate tectonic of the construction is internalized and masked by layers of smooth concrete. This project attempts to reveal that hidden tectonic by collapsing the stratified layers of skin, structure and texture into a single material—all visible and all functional.

The premise of this critique on construction looks specifically at the Taichung Opera House by Toyo Ito as a counterpoint precedent to fuel the discussion of the desire to reveal the hidden tectonic of forms that exhibit similar kinds of 3-dimensional spatial complexity. Though this particular precedent does not utilize similar classes of mathematical surface geometry, it is a relevant example of how a composition of curved walls could be organized into a rational structure-and-construction system. More importantly in our case, however, it is a good example of the stratified and cumbersome construction sequence associated with these kinds of forms using more traditional building methods. In this example, the construction sequence is broken down into four main steps: 1) a mesh of steel beams lays the foundation for the curved walls; 2) a finer steel mesh that shapes the walls and adds support for the concrete; 3) shotcrete (spray-on concrete) is applied to form the general massing; and 4) a layer of hand-plastered concrete adds the finish layer and desired texture.

Our process is driven largely by the pure geometric definition of the surfaces we explored, whereby the initial layer of ruling lines (glass-fiber) generate both the surface membrane and function as the soft fibrous mold for the additional layer of structural (carbon) fiber.

In this state, the mold is subject to deformation by the layering of geodesic curves along the soft glass-fiber surface. The aggregation of structural bays constructed both individually and in hybrid forms allows for the utilization of the glass-fiber mold in its hard state (post-resin application). This allows the carbon-fiber to trace geodesic curves along principal stress lines on the surface, acting as both a bonding agent and supplementary structural layer in parts of the surface experiencing maximum stress and potential deflection.

The series of explorations that led to the final product developed from an interest in doubly ruled surfaces. The majority of our early experiments looked into the hyperboloid of revolution as a doubly ruled anticlastic surface that operated within a closed and highly constrained system. The development of the project was a reciprocal dialogue between the role and function of the rigid scaffold (constructed out of plexiglass for the cotton-thread scale models), and the fiber layup algorithm. The focus of the development tested the limits of the rigid scaffold and the extent to which it was able to produce a varied range of forms (through algorithm variation), as well as its ability to extract specific desired characteristics of the geometries they produced. For example, one major development we achieved through the redesigning of the scaffold was the ability to lay geodesics on both sides of the surface, allowing for greater surface rigidity and strength. This was a multistep process that involved the re-thinking of the hyperboloid as the building block, whereby a calibrated sampling of the surface along its generating lines produced a module representative of a quarter of the fully revolved surface. In doing so, we were able to integrate a larger portion of the rigid scaffold into the surface generation for additional fiber attachment.

The generation of the hyperboloid module of varying eccentricities (degrees) was defined algorithmically by a given "skip count" of the list of pins on the rigid scaffold. Initial studies demonstrated the ability to produce hyperboloids of different eccentricities using identical rigid scaffolds. All of these models were woven by hand due to the desire to weave along the interior of the scaffold which would be inaccessible by the robotic arm. White cotton-thread was used for the initial layer of fiber (representative of glass-fiber). This formed the membrane and was generated from the two sets of ruling lines of the hyperbolic surface. Red cotton-thread represented the additional layers of carbon-fiber, and took the form of geodesic curves as supported by the fibrous mold of the white layer.

This sequence formed the basis of the concept of utilizing fiber as mold, whereby the initial layering of ruling lines became both the primitive definition of the mathematical surface tectonically and structurally, and the membrane onto which additional layers of fiber could be laid.

The final product was a series of spatial morphologies that demonstrated a varied range of aggregation techniques, module orientation, scale and type (wall/partition morphology, structural canopy and long span bridge). By assigning a specific scale and orientation to the module aggregations, we were able to embed a higher degree of specificity in the laying of carbon-fiber as the secondary and tertiary structural layers. We used a surface structural analysis tool in Millipede, a Grasshopper Plugin, to analyze the Von Mises stresses, and measure the deflection-under-load for each of the aggregations. Through these tests, we generated stress patterns on the surface and attempted to match the laying of carbon-fiber along principal stress lines while maintaining the geometric integrity of the surface (finding a best-fit solution between our algorithm and the directionality of the stress lines). This ensured that the two systems were visually cohesive.

The desire to utilize the surface as a hard mold after the resin had been applied to the initial layers demanded an integrated design of the scaffold and attachment mechanism. The layer of carbon-fiber that defined the principal stress lines of the surface was laid last (over the already hardened glass-fiber surface). In order to provide an edge condition that allowed for the addition of fiber to the module once the rigid scaffold had been removed, we embedded plastic tubing around the screws to which the first layers of glass-fiber were attached. This allowed for the clean and facile removal of the screws along with the rigid MDF scaffold after the first layer of resin had been applied, but left the surface with pieces of hardware on the edges that became both an attachment mechanism between hardened modules as well as pins for the final layer of carbon-fiber.

The spatial morphologies we developed were unspecific in programmatic definition. The ambition of the project was to present an idea about how a seemingly hermetic system can adapt to highly specific conditions relating to scale, orientation, load, and complex spatial organization.

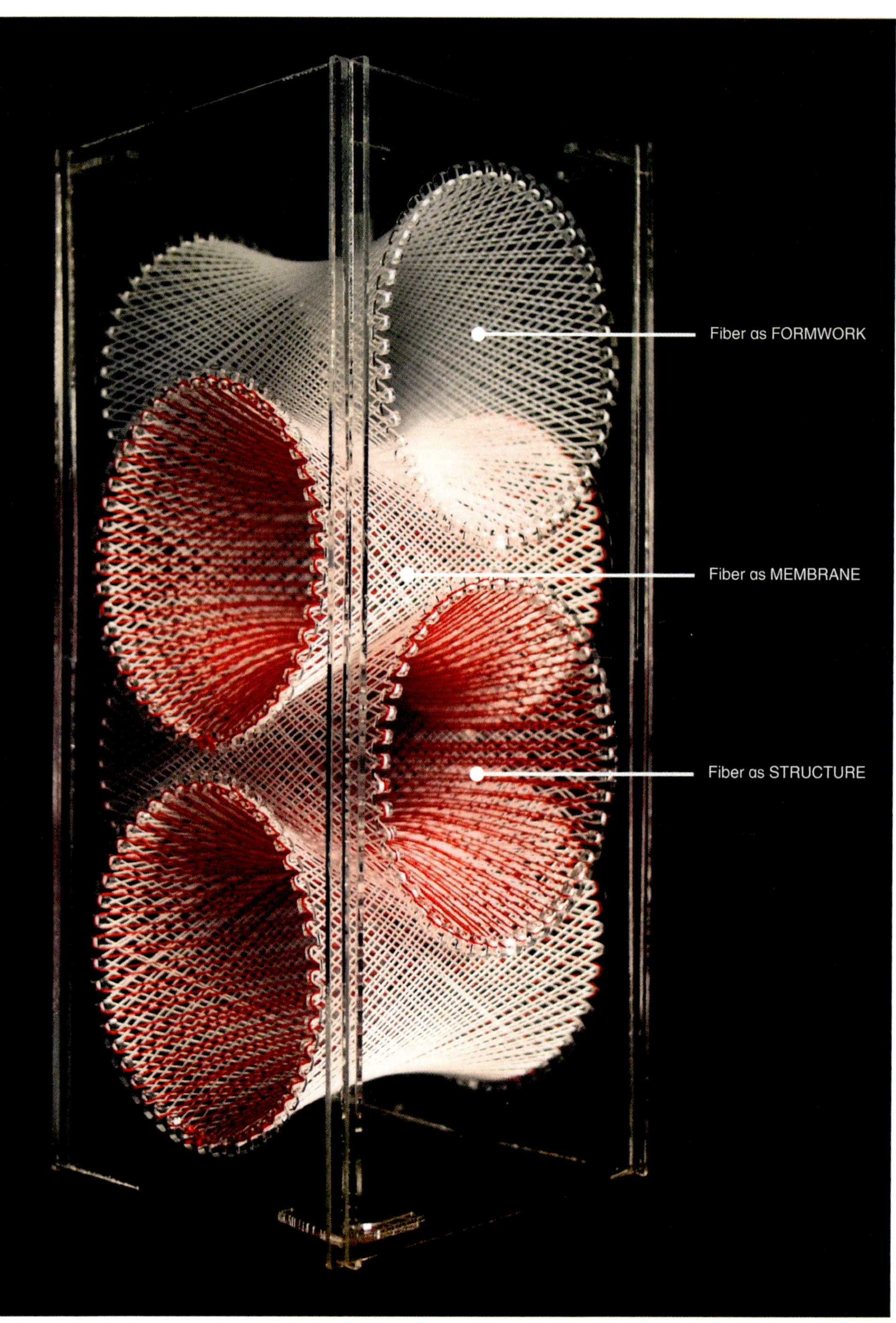






Fibrous-mold investigation of formwork, membrane, and structure.

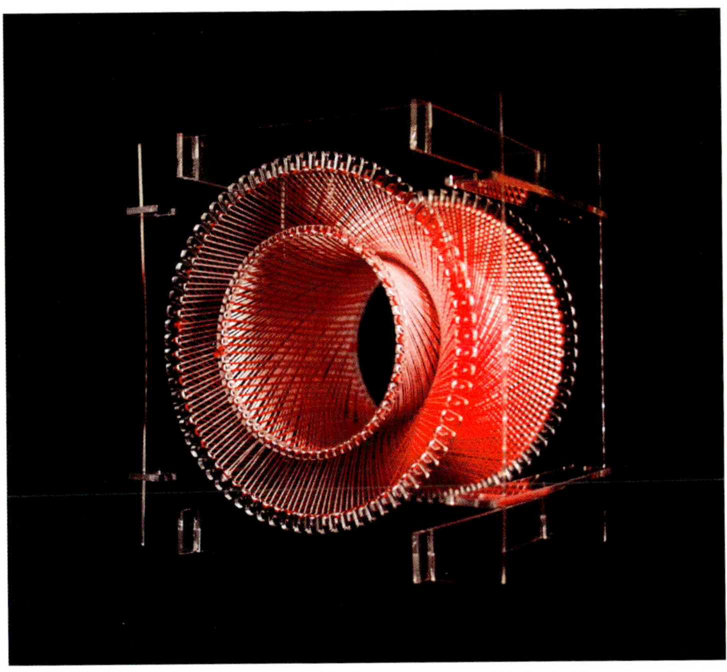

Investigations into intersection as part of the hyperboloid series.

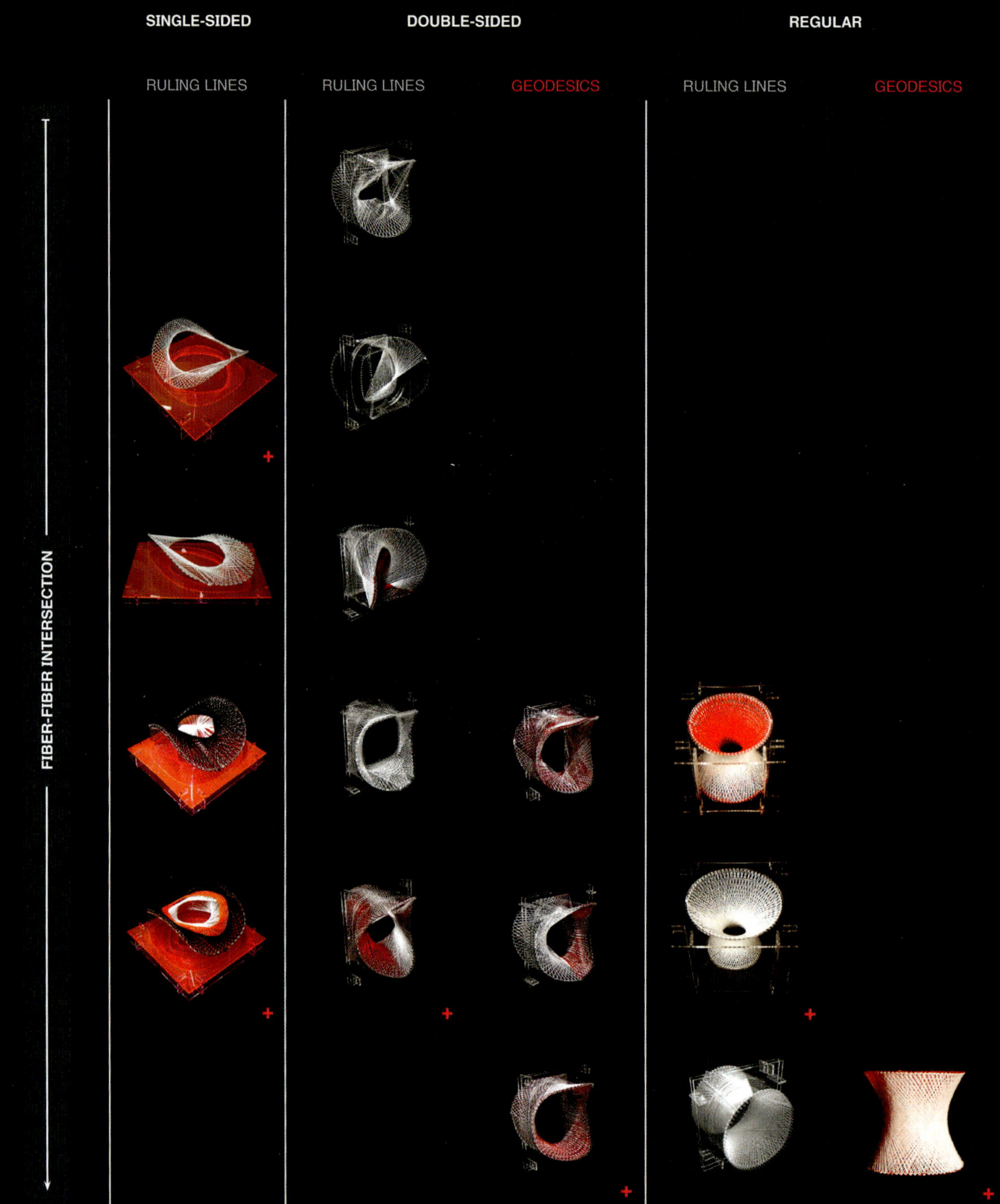


Matirx organizing intial investigations into cylindrical interactions and hyperboloids by fiber-to-fiber intersection.

HYPERBOLOID SERIES

SHEARED / TWISTED

INTERSECTIONS

AGGREGATIONS

| SHEARED / TWISTED | | INTERSECTIONS | | AGGREGATIONS | |
|---|---|---|---|---|---|
| INES | GEODESICS | RULING LINES | GEODESICS | RULING LINES | GEODESICS |

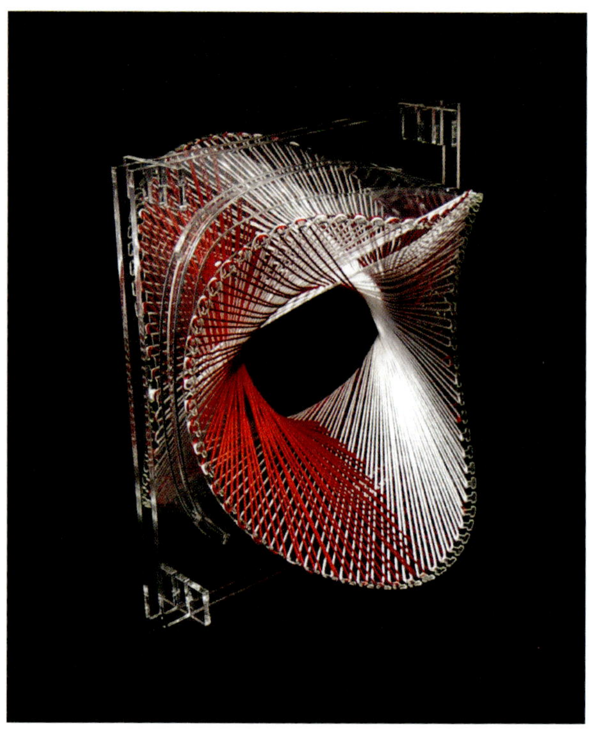

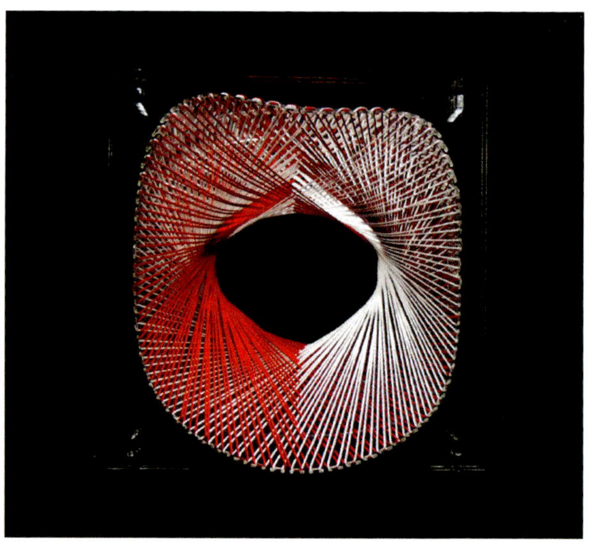

Double-sided cylindrical investigations
showing ruling lines and geodesics.

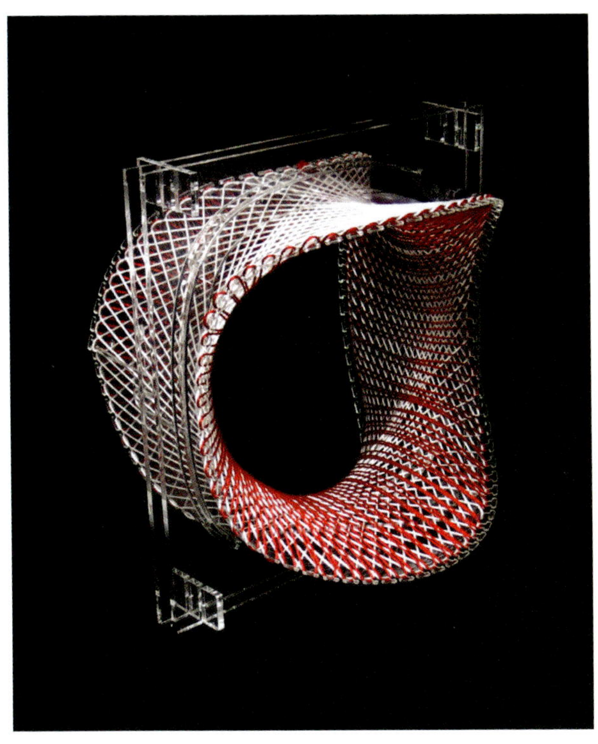

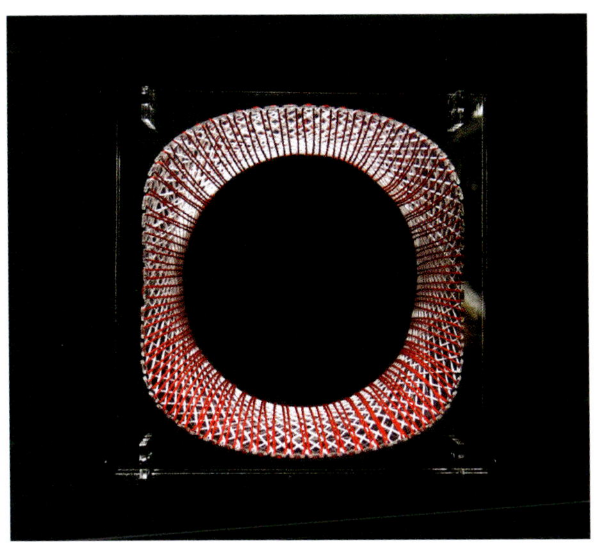

Double-sided cylindrical investigations
showing ruling lines and geodesics.

Above: Details of aggregation study within the hyperboloid series.

Following page: Aggregation study model within the hyperboloid series.

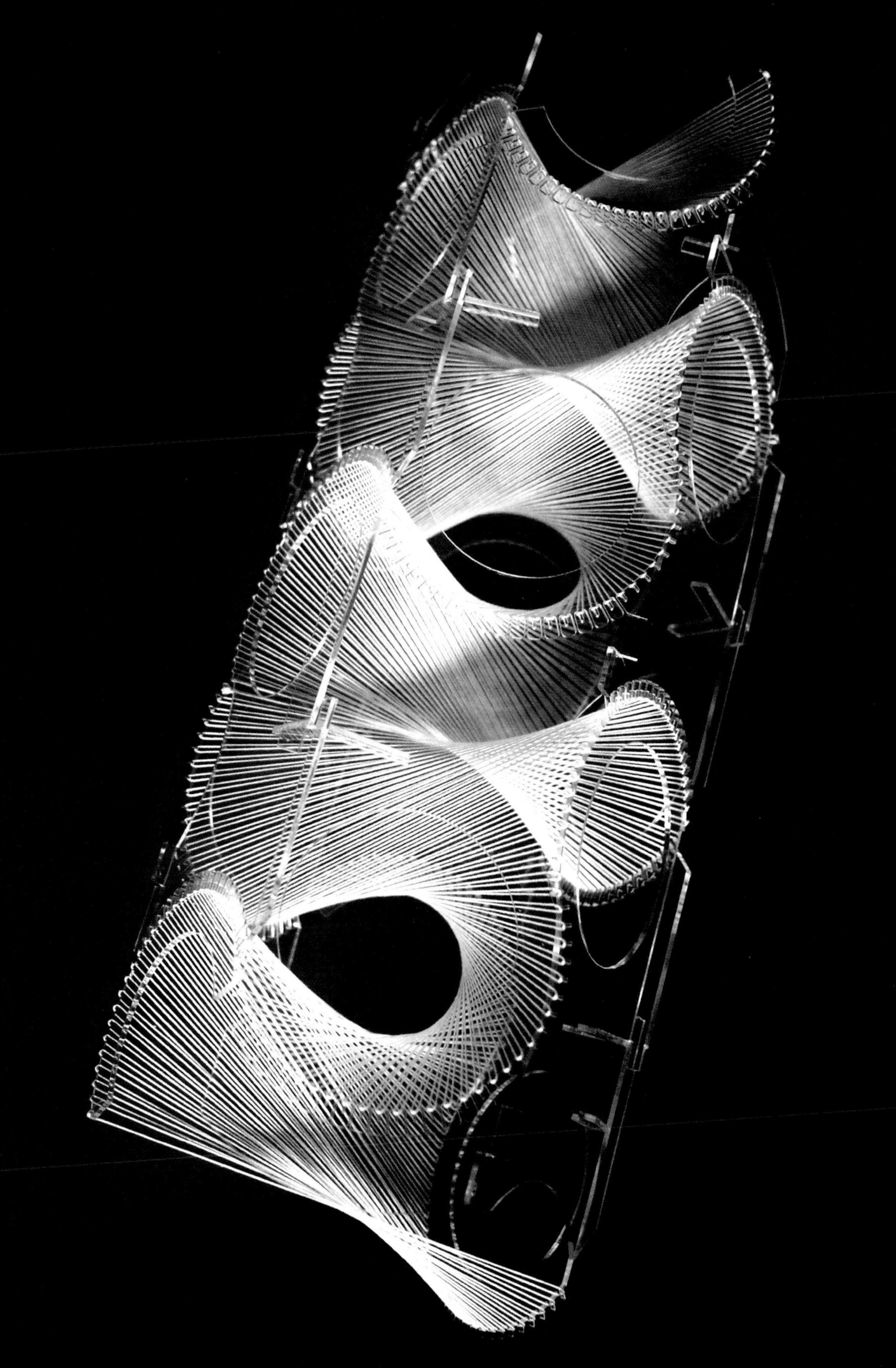

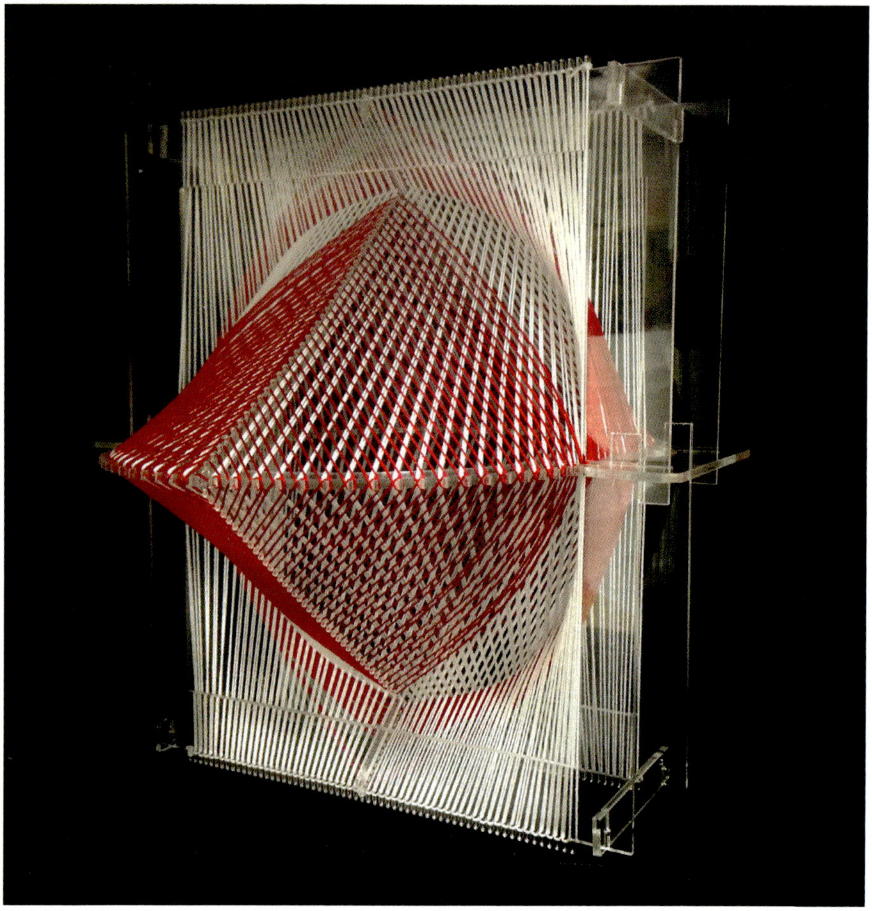

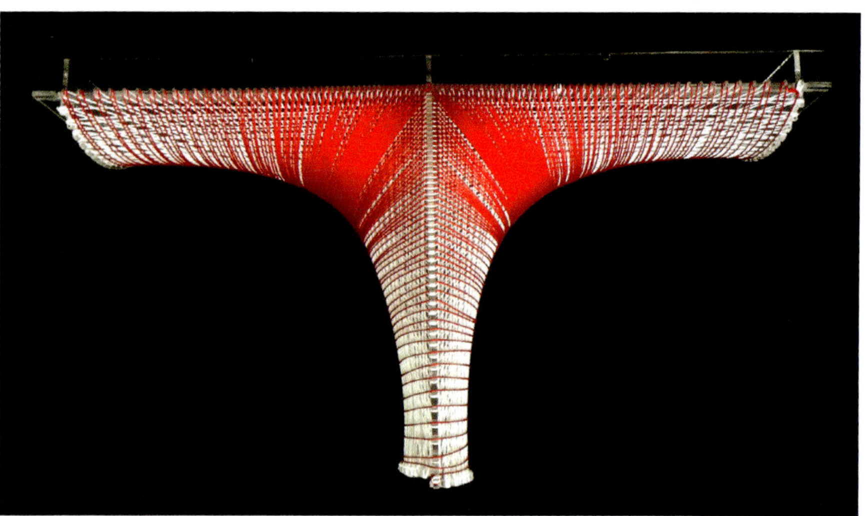

Top and bottom: Module aggregation study models.

Following page: Detail of mirrored module aggregation study.

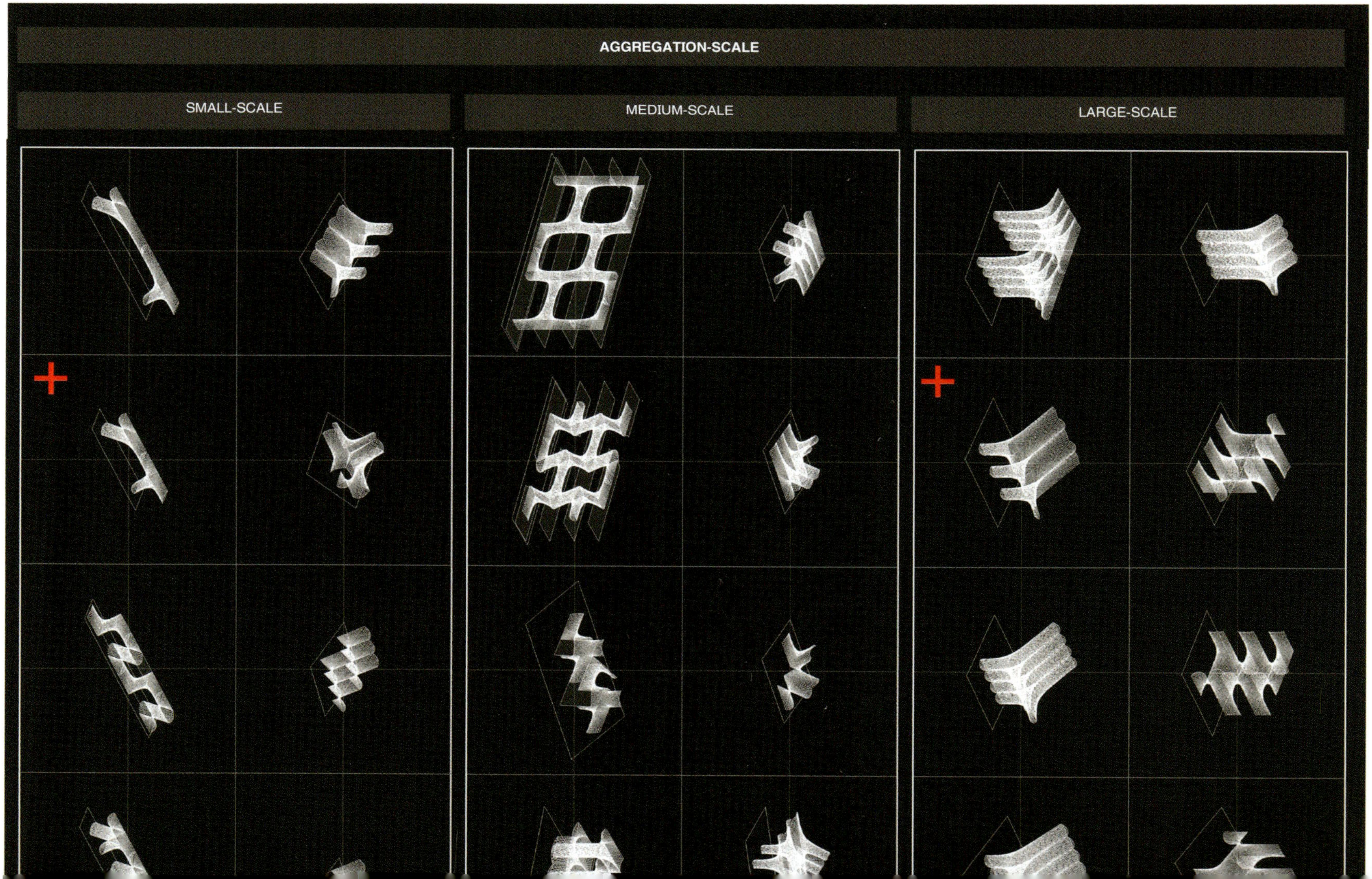

AGGREGATION-SCALE

SMALL-SCALE

MEDIUM-SCALE

LARGE-SCALE

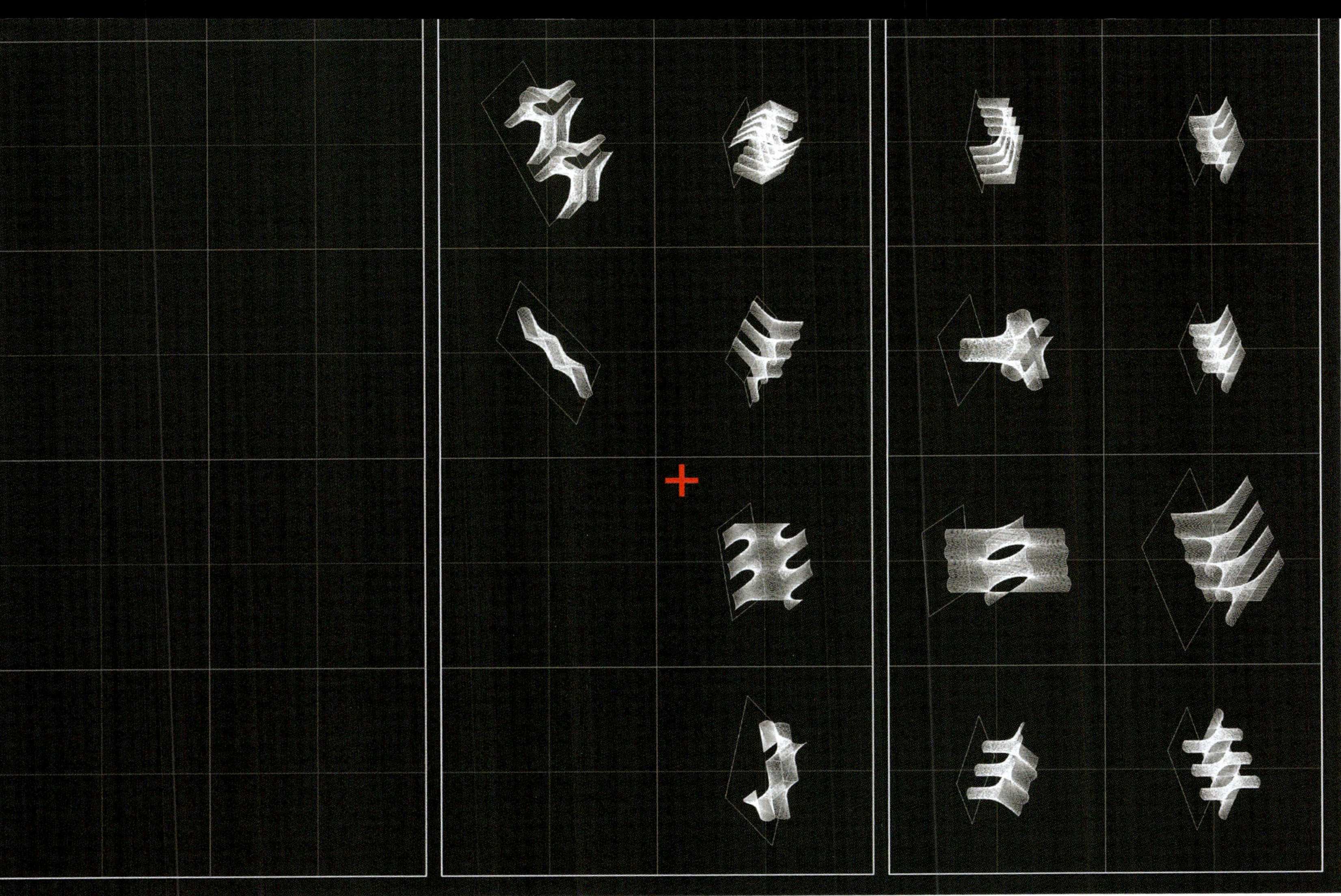

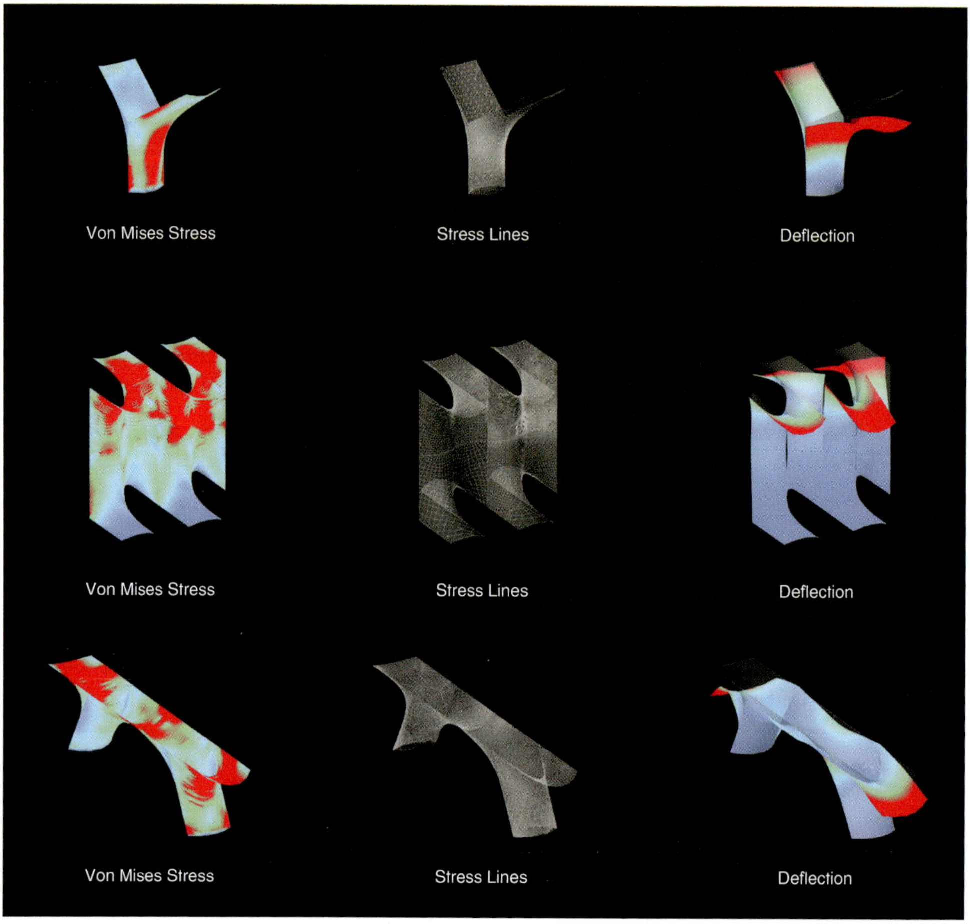

Von Mises Stress

Stress Lines

Deflection

Von Mises Stress

Stress Lines

Deflection

Von Mises Stress

Stress Lines

Deflection



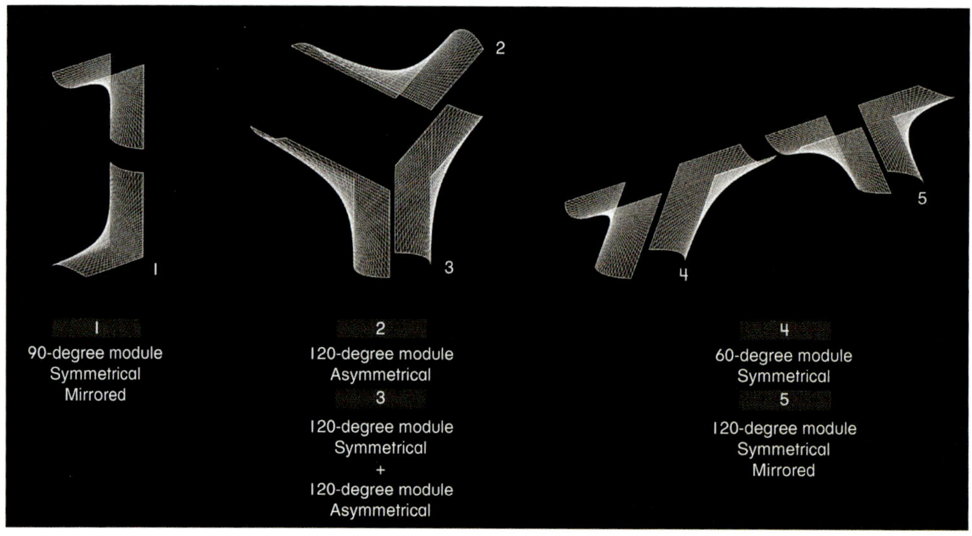


Previous spread: Matrix of rotated module aggregation studies.

Top: Structural analysis of selected modules from the rotated aggregation series.

Bottom: Diagram of form investigations of selected aggregation module, using symmetrical, asymemetrical, and mirrored rotation.

Process and assembly images of carbon-fiber spatial morphology models.

Model of spatial-morphology aggregation 01 of wall typology.

Top: Model of spatial-morphology aggregation 02 of structural canopy.

Bottom: Model of spatial-morphology aggregation 03 of long-span enclosure.

# An Architectonic Notion for Knitting and Pneumatics

Yuan Gao
Demir Purisic
Zahra Safaverdi
Joseph Varholick



The fibrous tectonics studio investigates new methodologies, arrangements, and applications of composite-fiber materials, namely carbon-and-glass-fibers which are saturated in epoxy resin. The aim of the investigation is to propose an innovative system of deploying these specific materials.

Our system combines the traditional textile technique of knitting with inflatable pneumatic membranes to create composite-fiber structures. We see these two techniques as inherently complementary. The pneumatic membrane is able to pretension the fibers of the knit surface and expand it into a spatial- and form-active volume while knitting allows the fibrous surface to be behaviorally and topologically programmed, which, in turn, determines how the pneumatic membrane inflates. The resulting configuration of fibers is then saturated with resin and cured into a rigid structure.

This system addresses three major issues in the contemporary application of composite-fibers. First, composite-fibers today are most often applied as a homogenous, anisotropic surface. Fibers are woven into regular textiles or cut and sprayed in a random (approximately homogenous) configuration. This is a misuse of fibers which have definite isotropic properties and should be deployed efficiently (i.e. not homogeneously, but where loads [or aesthetics] dictate). Second, conventional processes compromise the continuity (and furthermore the structural integrity) of fibers by cutting textiles into templates or use cutto-length fibers in spray applications. The result of these processes are often components that are joined using alien hardware (nuts and bolts). Third, almost all fibers are deployed with the use of a mold or mandrel or scaffold. These aids to production require significant material investment often surpassing the cost of fibers and resin (unless production number per mold is high) and limit the complexity and variety of forms produced.

Although the exploration of fibrous-composites such as carbon-fiber and fiberglass is relatively new (1930s), the history of fibrous tectonics is ancient. The notion of making with a fibrous material is heavily rooted in textile traditions. Knitting takes advantage of the anisotropic (and otherwise specific) nature of fibers and is capable of deploying material in a highly programmed heterogeneous arrangement, allowing the designer to control both form and material behavior.

Knitting is an inherently programmable process. The algorithm which informs stitches may allow for a variety of patterns. Alternating the pattern, density, or tension of stitches results in a fabric surface with specific behavioral properties. Elasticity or rigidity, density or porosity can be programmed into the material via geometric arrangement. In this way a highly inelastic material (carbon-fiber) can be rearranged at a tectonic scale to mimic otherwise alien material properties (elasticity). This geometric elasticity can be witnessed in most looseknit clothing. For example, a scarf can have much more elastic than an individual length of yarn from which it is knit. Knitting as a fabrication process allows for material to be deployed in an extremely heterogeneous and specific arrangement, contrasting the homogenous and anisotropic application of conventional processes.

Unlike other textile techniques, knitting uses a single, continuous fiber. Composites function best when fibers are continuous. This configuration of continuous, interlocking loops has the added benefit of allowing the fiber to be easily recycled. Knitting also controls the profile of the resulting surface through the stitch pattern. This contrasts methods such as weaving, where looms are often set to produce rectangular lengths of fabric which are then cut into templates to be assembled, compromising the continuity and integrity of fibers at the edges.Knit surfaces may have complex profiles and topologies where fibers are always continuous at the edge.

Formal and structural investigations led to the modeling of complex forms and topologies. These would often be approximated by joining several knit-textile surfaces which were produced separately. An incredible benefit of the process is that separate knit surfaces may be continuous/seamless when joined. Stitches identical to those used in the production of the fabric surface may be used to close seams, ultimately creating a uniform condition. Locating seams appropriately allows for complex geometry to be unrolled into manufacturable templates with minimal distortion. Additional information such as stress mapping and load flows may be unrolled along with these surfaces, informing the template's knit algorithm in terms of density and pattern. Ultimately, complex configurations of fibers may be accomplished as tectonically continuous forms, improving upon processes that cut and compromise the integrity of fibers, and component-based systems that rely on alien hardware for aggregation or assembly.

Although knitting affords tremendous possibilities in the deployment of these materials, interacting fibers may only form a tensile surface, and therefore need a means of activation in order to be deployed as a tensioned volumetric forms. Fibers can be formed and tensioned within a mold or by winding fibers across the surface of a mandrel or scaffold. Our system investigates tensioning fibers via pneumatic bladders which are inflated inside a (closed) knit surface. Pneumatics require the least material investment per volume of any activation (i.e. forming and pre-tensioning) system and may be easily scaled.

Since the pneumatic membranes are relatively flexible and malleable, a single type of membrane can be manipulated into a variety of forms by a programmed, enclosing tensile surface. Regular standardized pneumatics can be arranged in a controlled way to achieve a variety of unique volumetric configurations. Complexity and uniqueness is a free consequence of the knitting algorithm. In other words, the pattern and topology with which a fibrous textile is knit will pre-determine the form, behavior, and configuration of the interacting pneumatics and fibers.

In conclusion, our system combines the traditional textile technique of knitting with inflatable pneumatic membranes to create composite-fiber structures. Knitting takes advantage of the anisotropic (and otherwise specific) nature of fibers and is capable of deploying material in a highly programmed heterogeneous arrangement, allowing the designer to (softly) control both form and material behavior. The techniques of knitting and pneumatic inflation are inherently complementary. The pneumatic membrane is able to pre-tension the fibers of the knit surface and expand it into a spatial and form-active volume while a knit surface may determine how the pneumatic membrane inflates and aggregates. Complexity and customization are therefore a free consequence of the algorithmic (and possibly automated) knitting process. This opens possibilities beyond the constraints of the traditional mold. We investigated how these processes allow for a continuous aggregation of fibers that do not rely on the traditional notion of joinery or hardware (which often produce structural weak points in composite structures). Lastly, all processes we have identified have counterparts at a much larger scale, and therefore invite the notion of a scalable system that can approach an architecture.

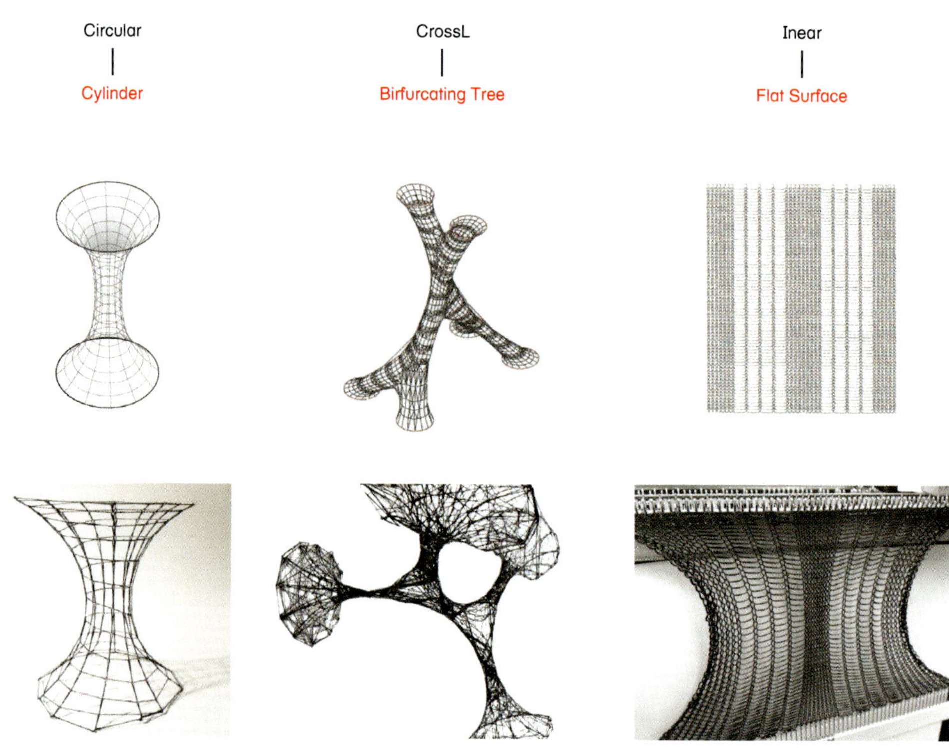




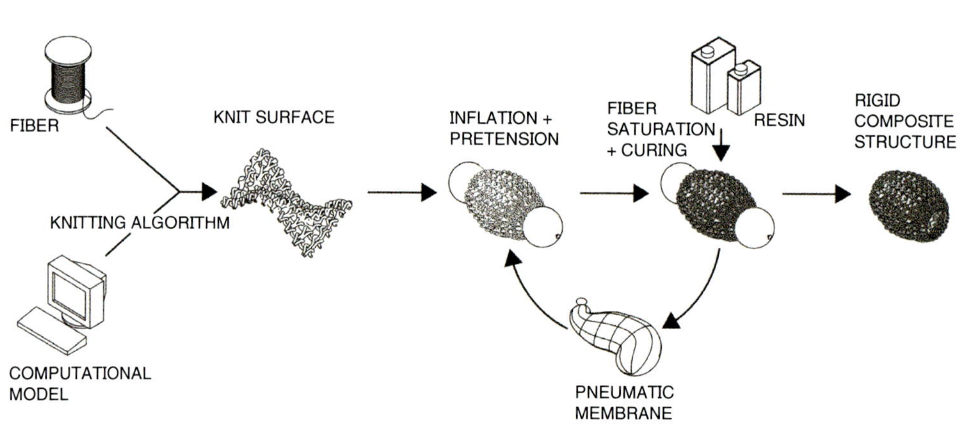




Top: Surface typologies developed from knitting looms.

Bottom: System combining traditional textile techniques of knitting with inflatable pneumatic membrances creating composite-fiber structures.

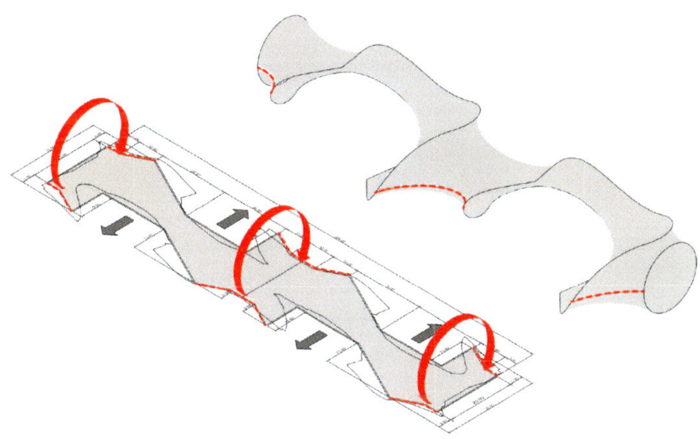

Top: Knitting machine used to create linear fabric that can be rolled into form.

Bottom: Diagram of unrolled fabric with edges idenitified to be joined at seams.

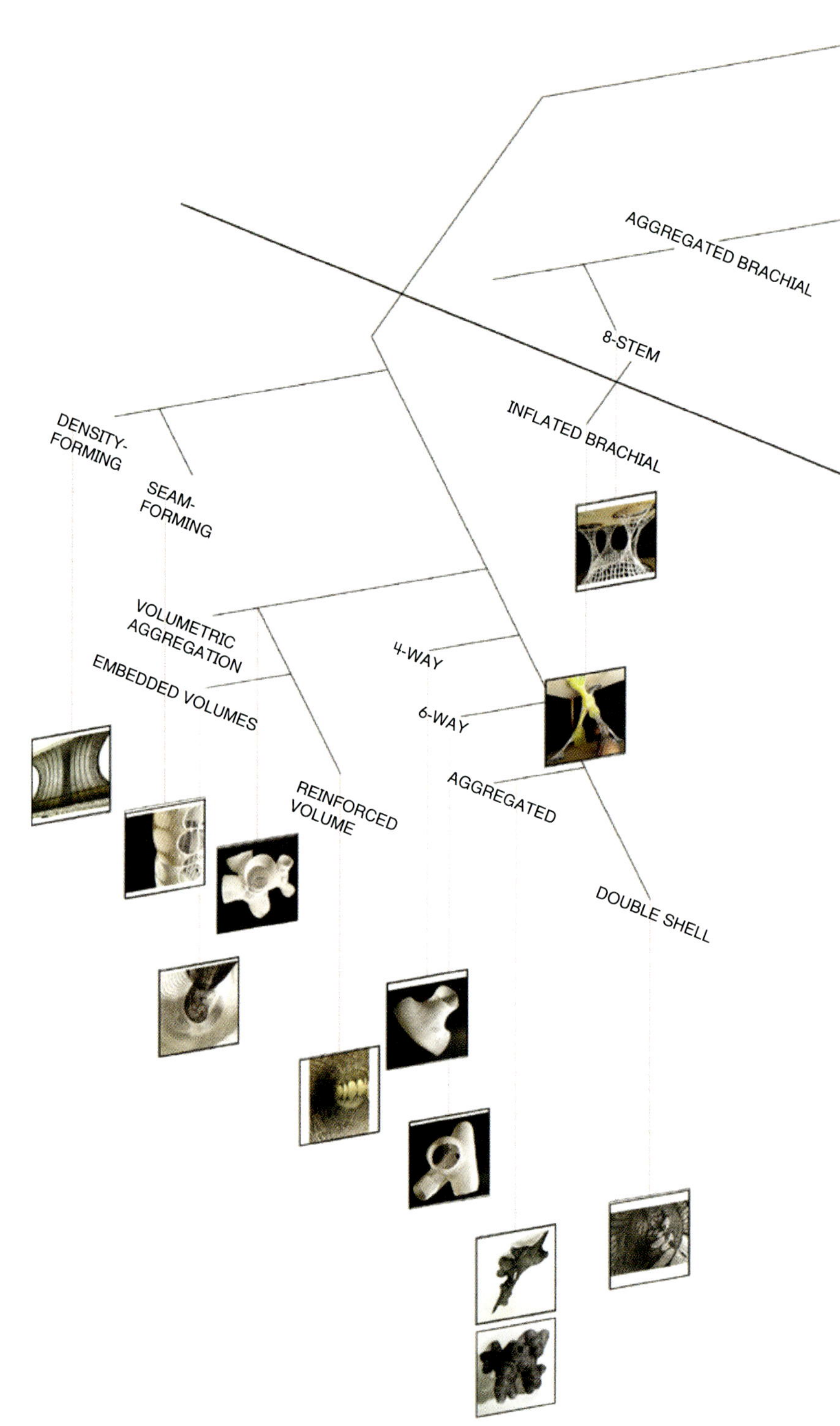
AGGREGATED BRACHIAL
8-STEM
INFLATED BRACHIAL
DENSITY-
FORMING
SEAM-
FORMING
VOLUMETRIC
AGGREGATION
EMBEDDED VOLUMES
4-WAY
6-WAY
REINFORCED
VOLUME
AGGREGATED
DOUBLE SHELL

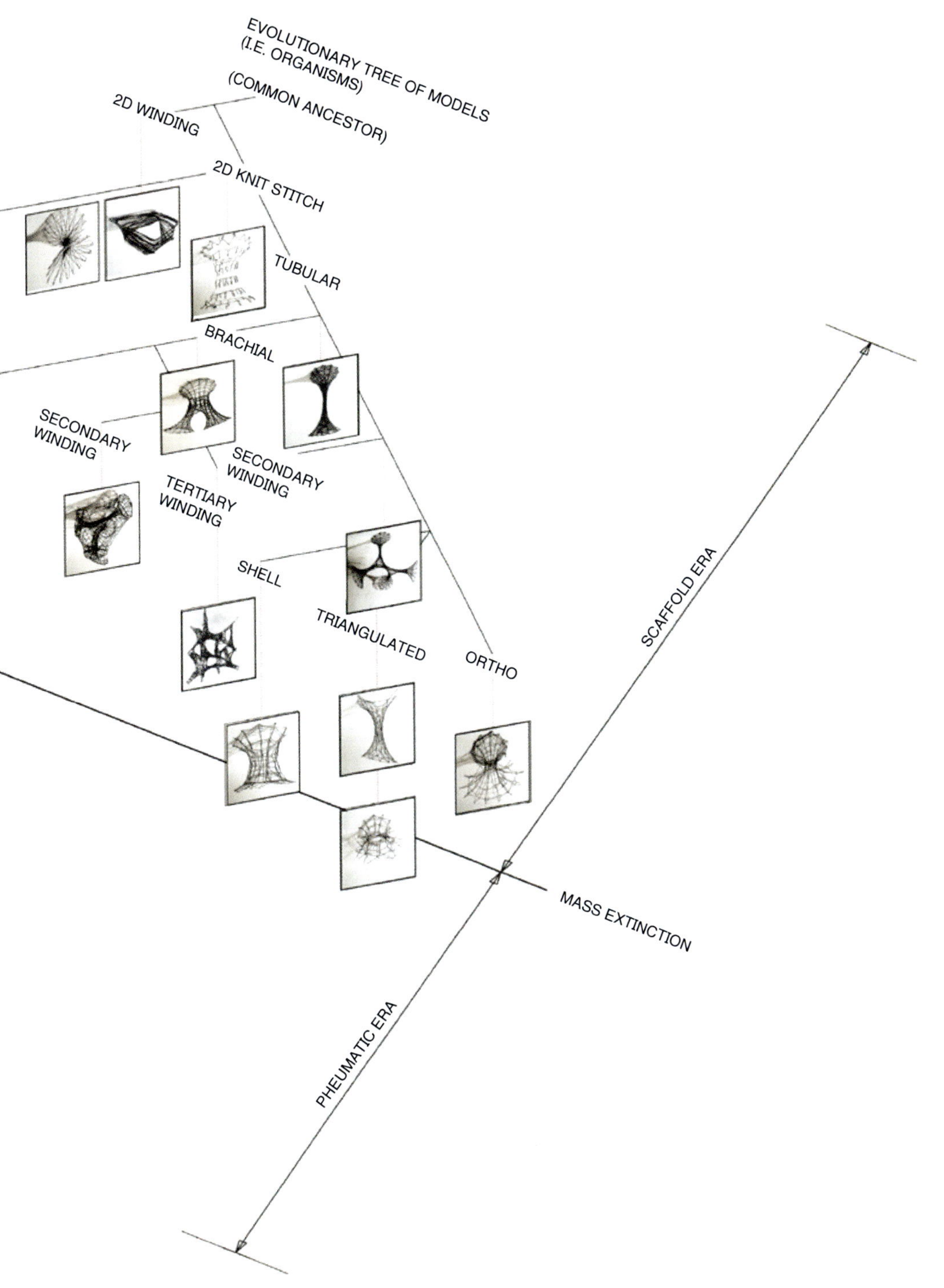


System matrix overview of experimentation showing the evolution of models.

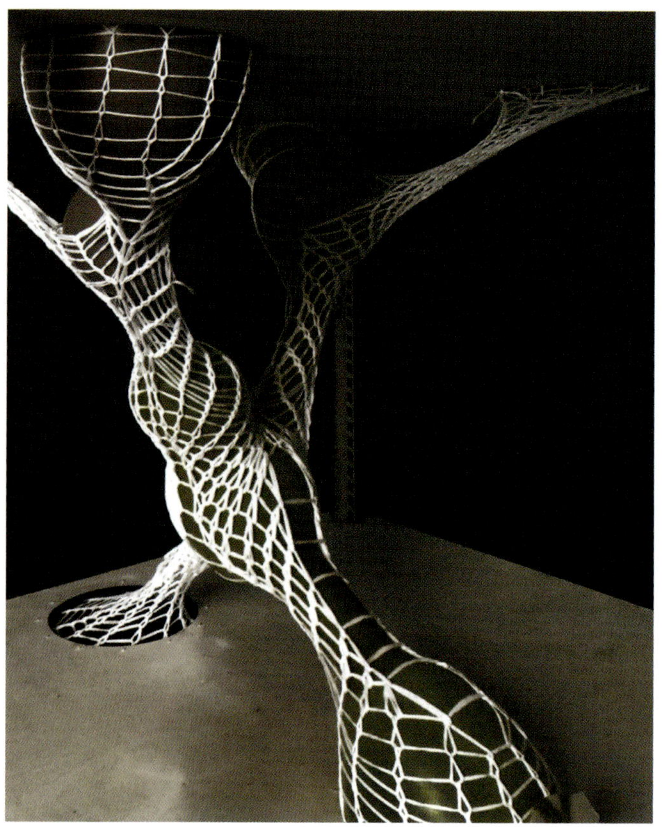

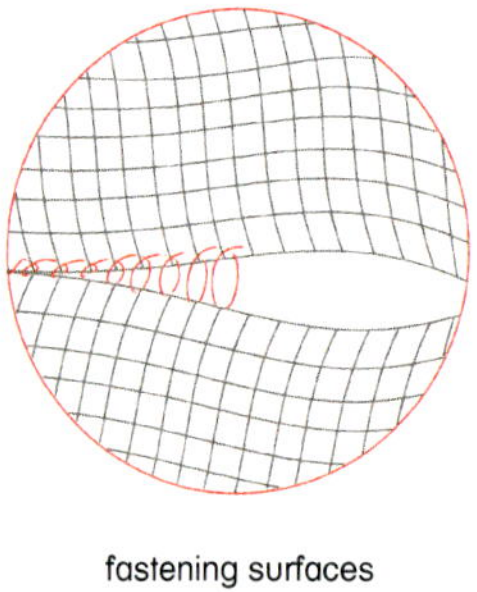


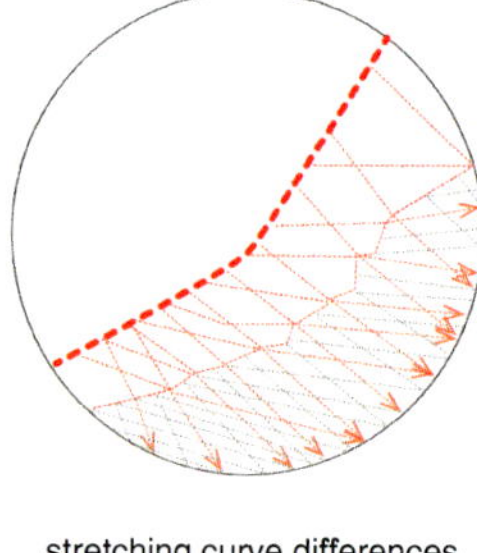


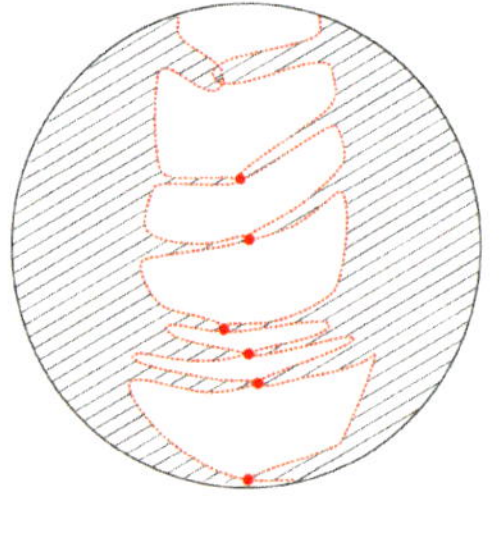




Top: Knitting study model with continuous aggregation.

Bottom: Model examples and diagrams of multiple-seam conditions developed.

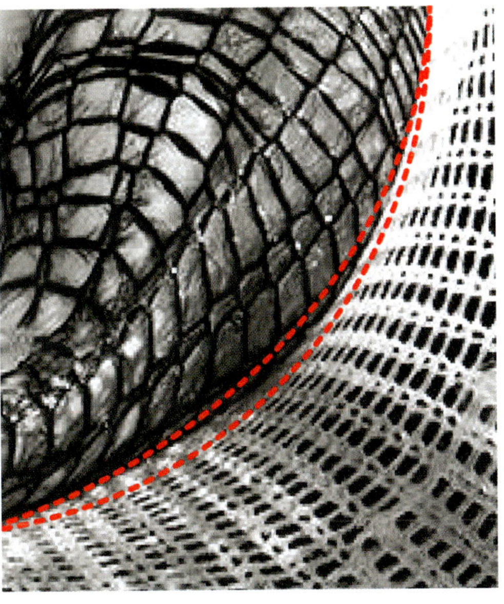

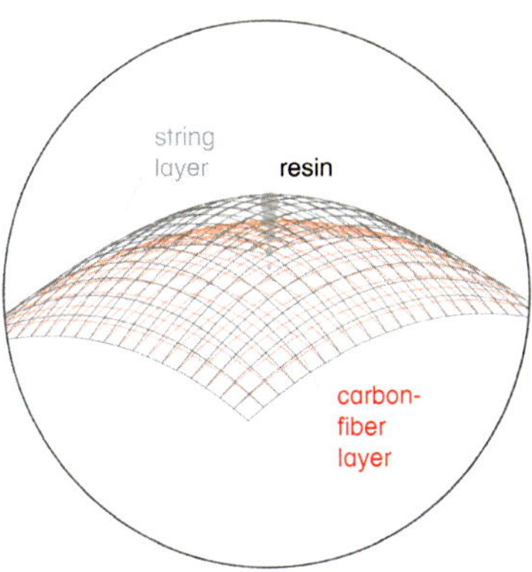


Top: Brachial structures of continous aggregation knitting showing possible arrangements of bifurcation.

Bottom: Textile heterogeneity of double-layered knitting system.

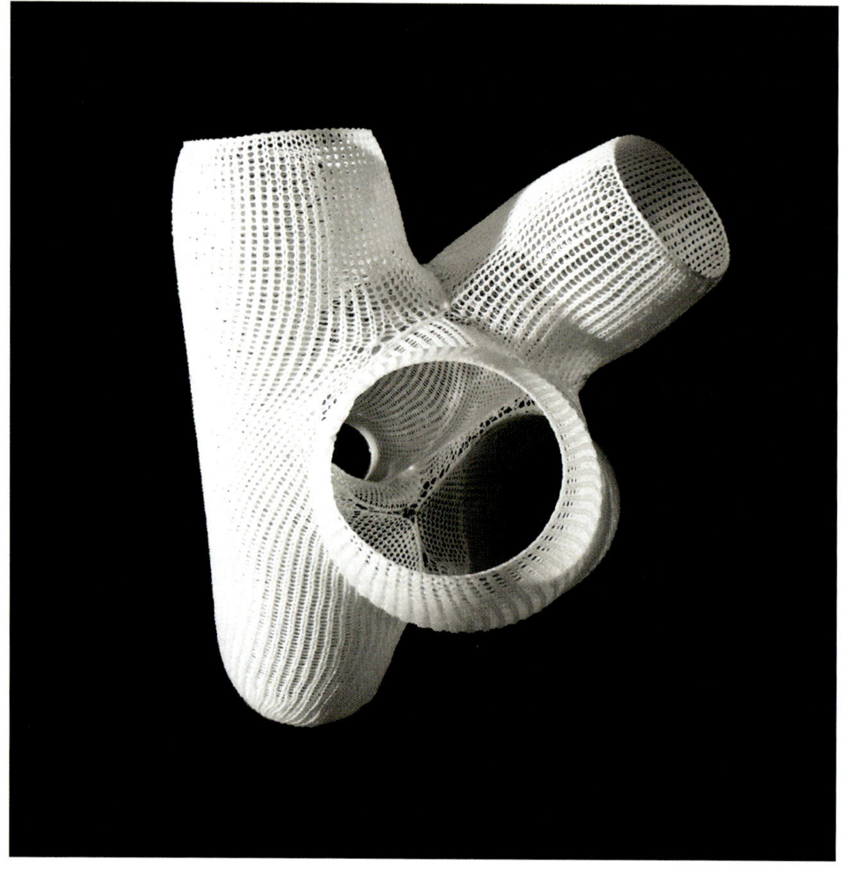





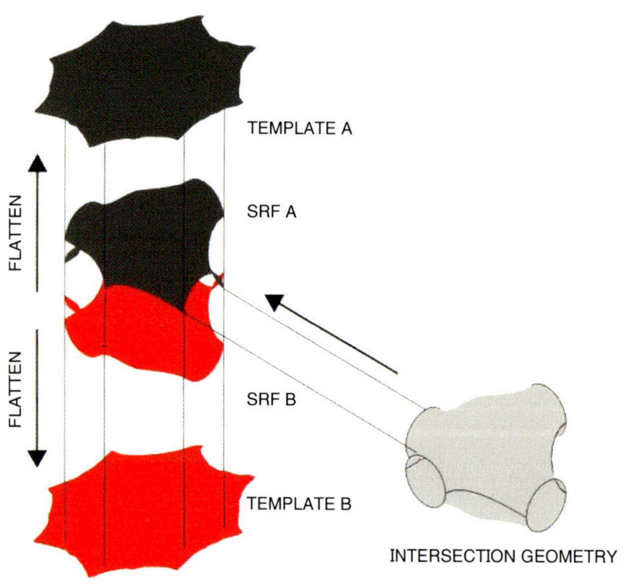


Top: Knitted model made of joined continuous strips.

Bottom: Diagram of developed surfaces and sutures that can be mapped across multiple geometries.

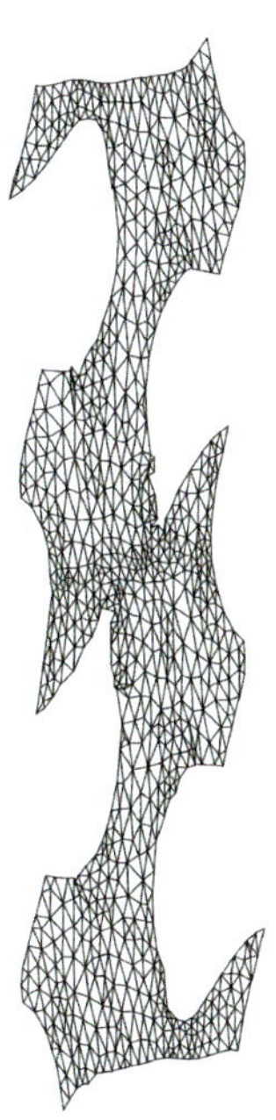

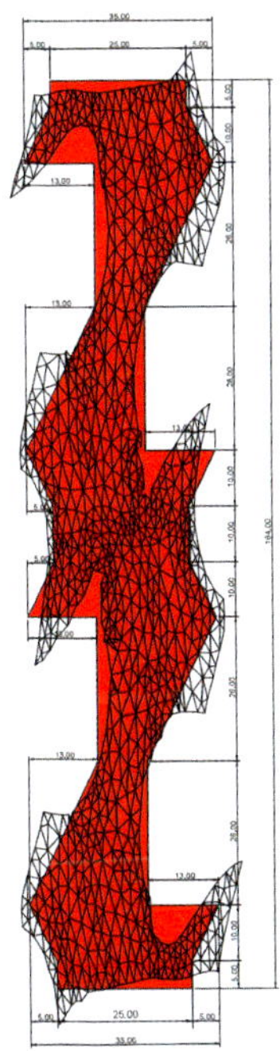

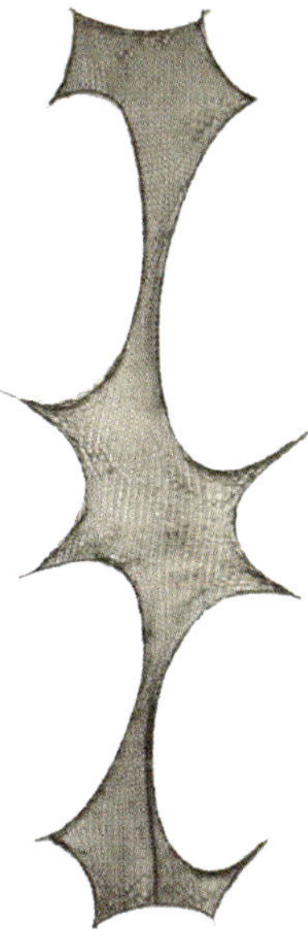

Top: Final instance model 1 with network bracing comprising two sets of points that define the double wall assembly surface.

Bottom: Development of sutured geometry unrolled to minimized deformation in 2D template.

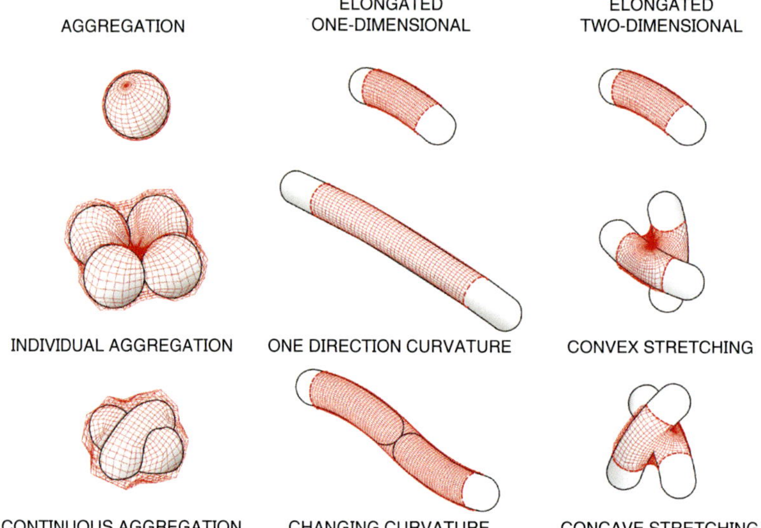


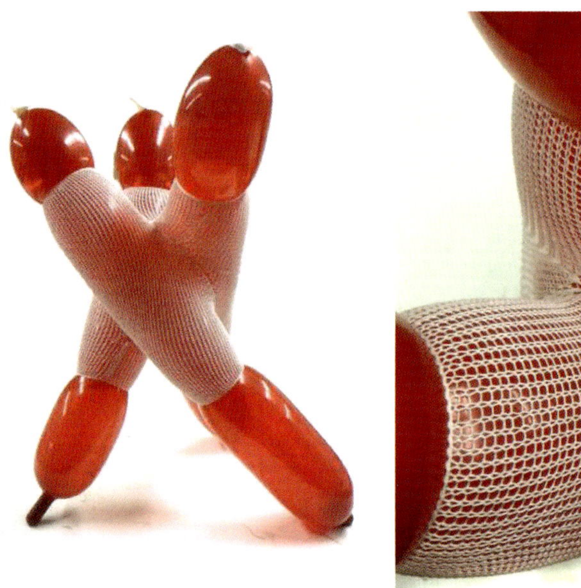

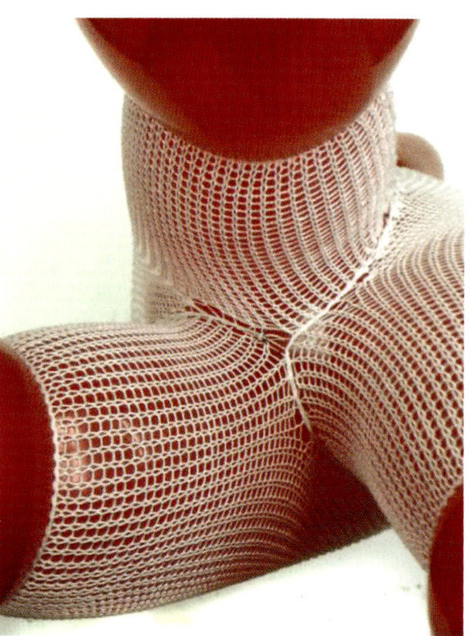

Top: Typology diagram of scalability and variation within the pneumatics system.

Bottom: Inflated models showing amorphous bladders that allow topology and local elasticity of the fibrous, knit surface to determine form.

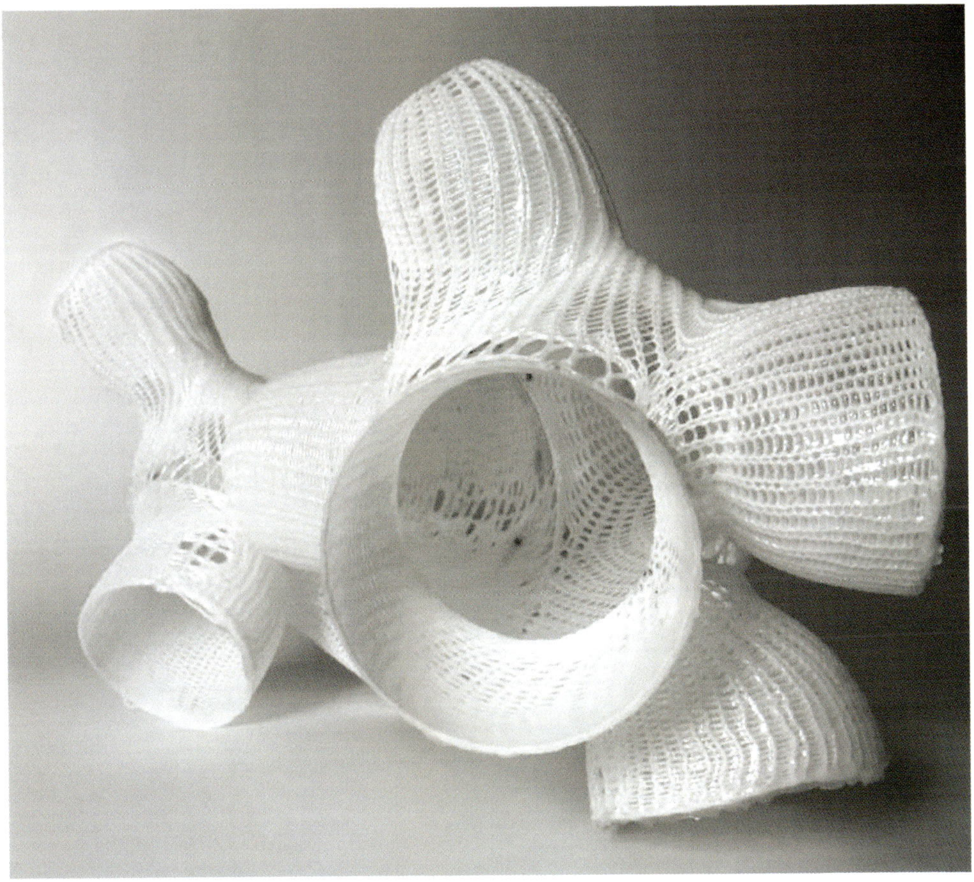

Top: Model showing connection between two “nodes” demonstrating interlocking of multiple continuous surfaces.

Bottom: Details of knitting composite-fiber structures without traditional joinery or fasteners.

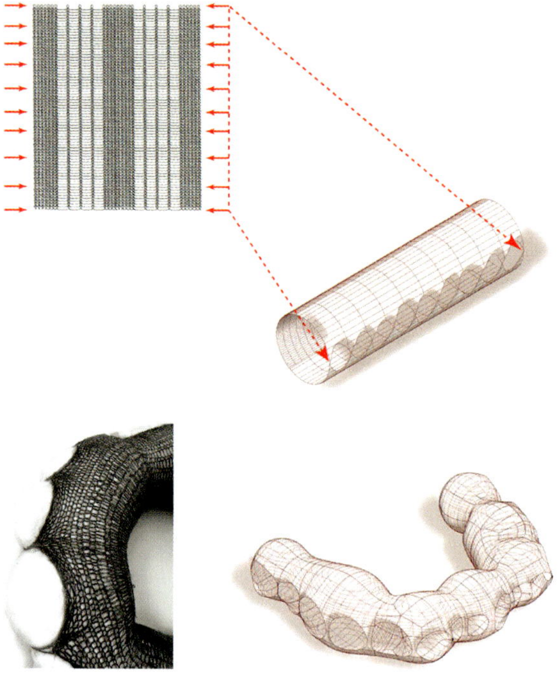

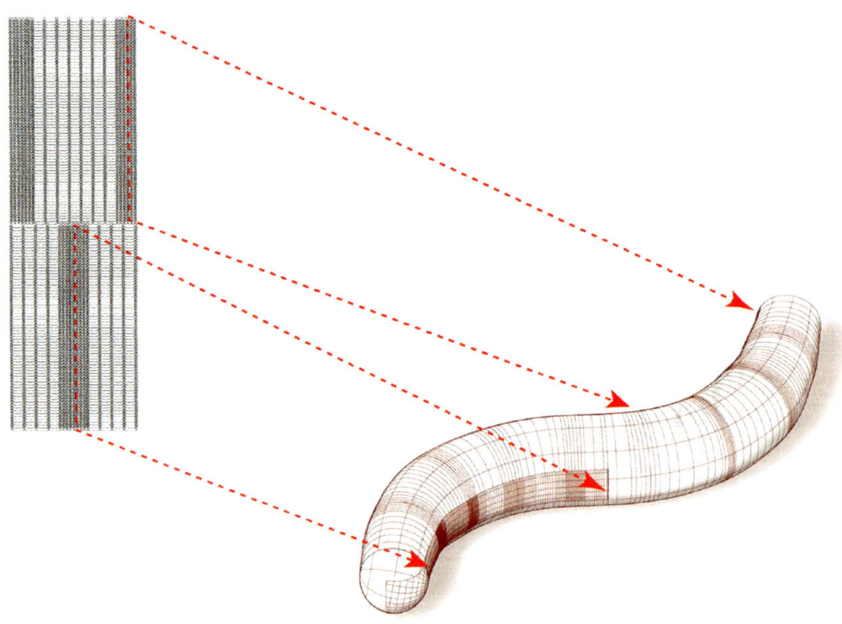

Top: Variations in knitting pattern and technique allows for different forms, appertures, and openings within the structure.

Bottom: Diagram of how code manipulations can establish variations in the formal algorithm.

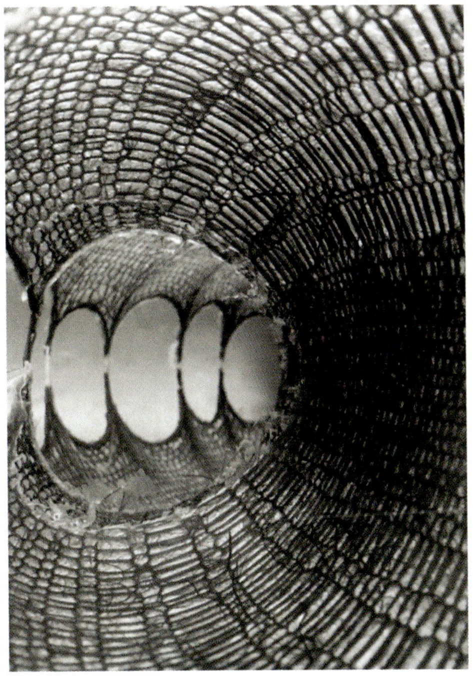

Model details demonstrating how forms can be embedded within one another using complex configurations of bladder and textiles.

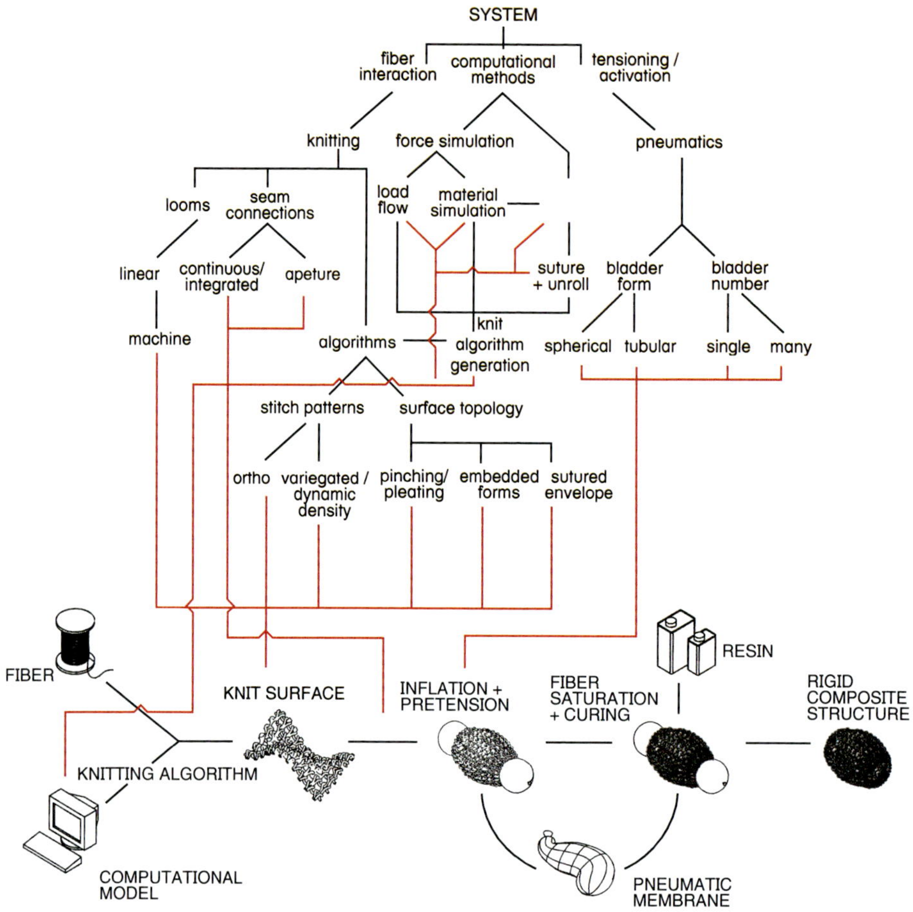

SYSTEM
fiber interaction
computational methods
tensioning / activation
knitting
force simulation
pneumatics
looms
seam connections
load flow
material simulation
linear
continuous/ integrated
apeture
suture + unroll
bladder form
bladder number
machine
algorithms
knit algorithm generation
spherical
tubular
single
many
stitch patterns
surface topology
ortho
variegated / dynamic density
pinching/ pleating
embedded forms
sutured envelope
FIBER
KNIT SURFACE
INFLATION + PRETENSION
FIBER SATURATION + CURING
RESIN
RIGID COMPOSITE STRUCTURE
KNITTING ALGORITHM
COMPUTATIONAL MODEL
PNEUMATIC MEMBRANE

Top: Final systems diagram of composite-sturcture process.

Bottom, left: Removal of bladder after resin has cured. All materials are incorporated into composite structure or are able to be reused.

Bottom, right: Detail of final instance model 1 without pneumatic membrane.

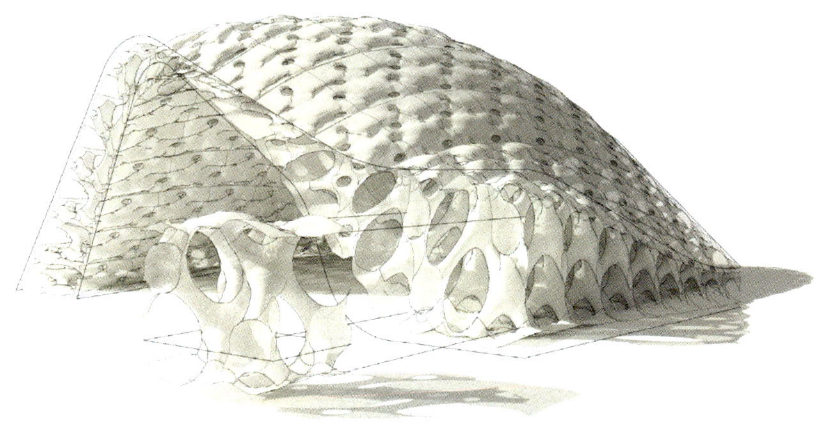

Top: Diagram of final instance model 1 showing incorporation of bracing of module in double wall.

Bottom: Proto-architectural concept of final instance model 1.

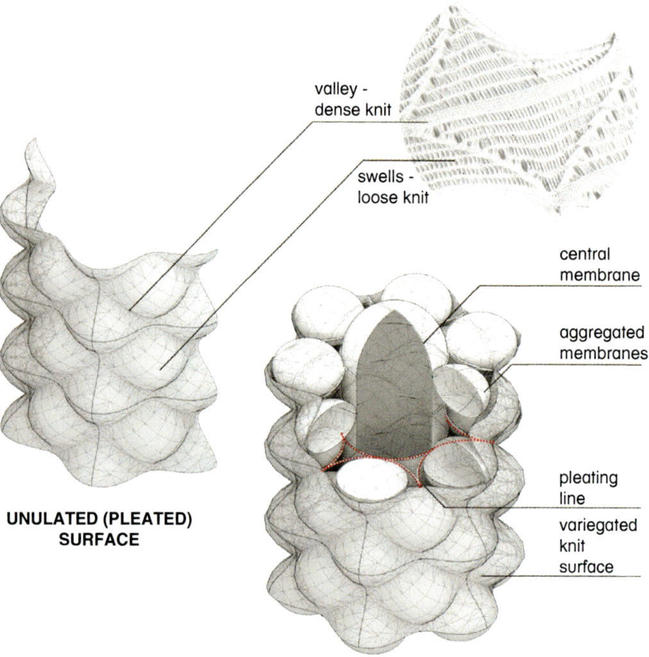




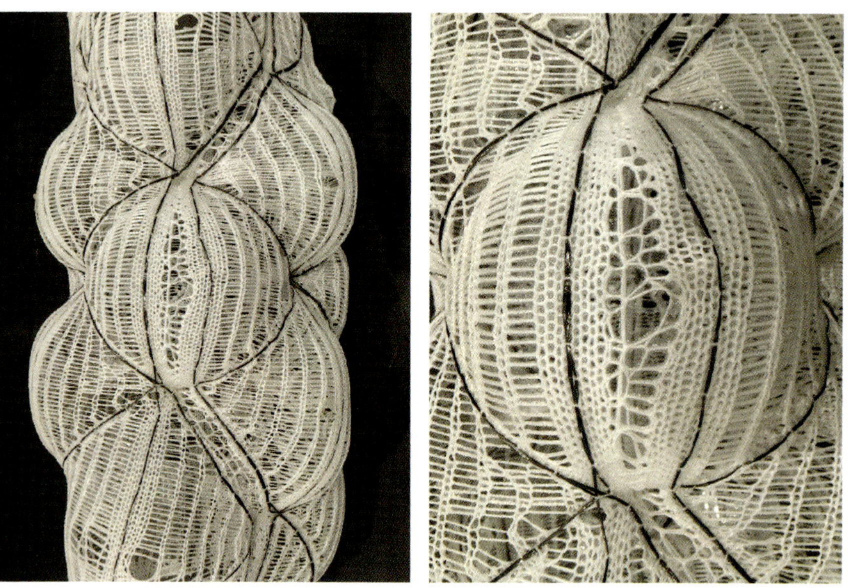



Top: Diagram of final instance model 2 showing pleating technique of wrapping a network of knit surfaces around an arrangement of pneumatic membranes.

Bottom: Details of final instance model 2 demonstrating embedding pleats into the form of the structural fibers.

**PROTO-ARCHITECTURAL FORM**

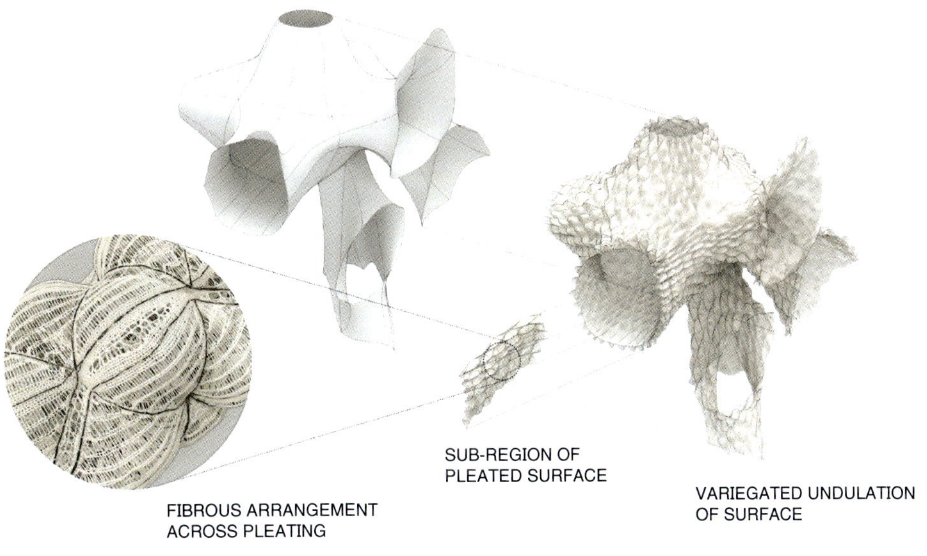

Top: Proto-architectural form created using final instance model 2 technique.

Bottom: Detail of final instance model 2 showing pleating of structural fibers.

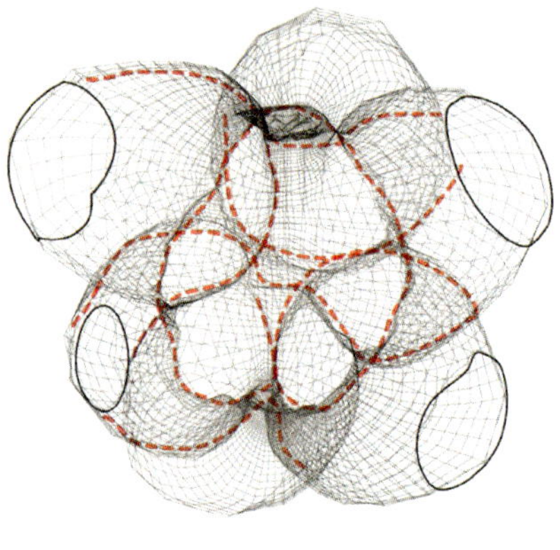

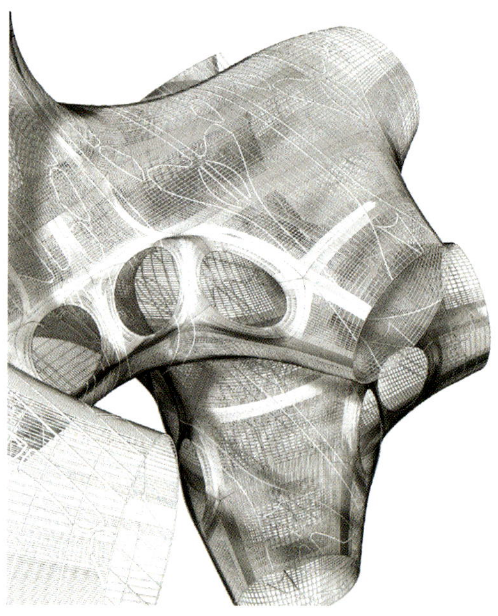

Top: Diagrams of final instance model 2 with embedded fibers in seams.

Bottom: Proto-architectural morphology with double shell structural qualities.

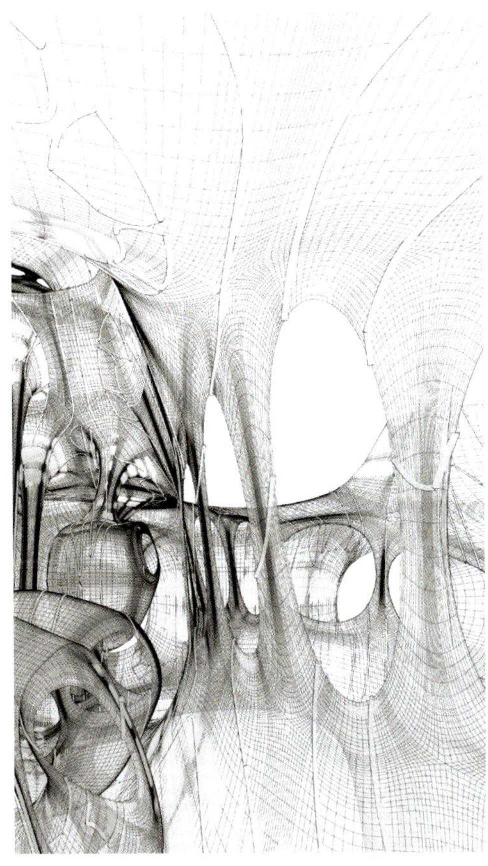

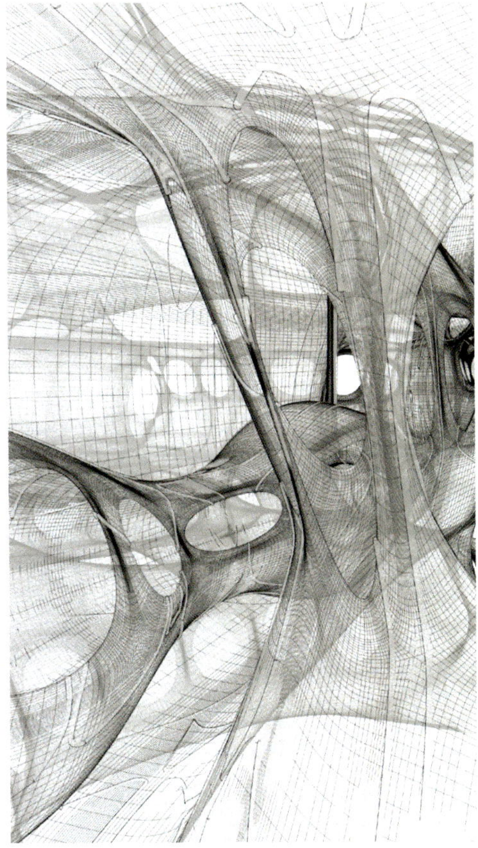





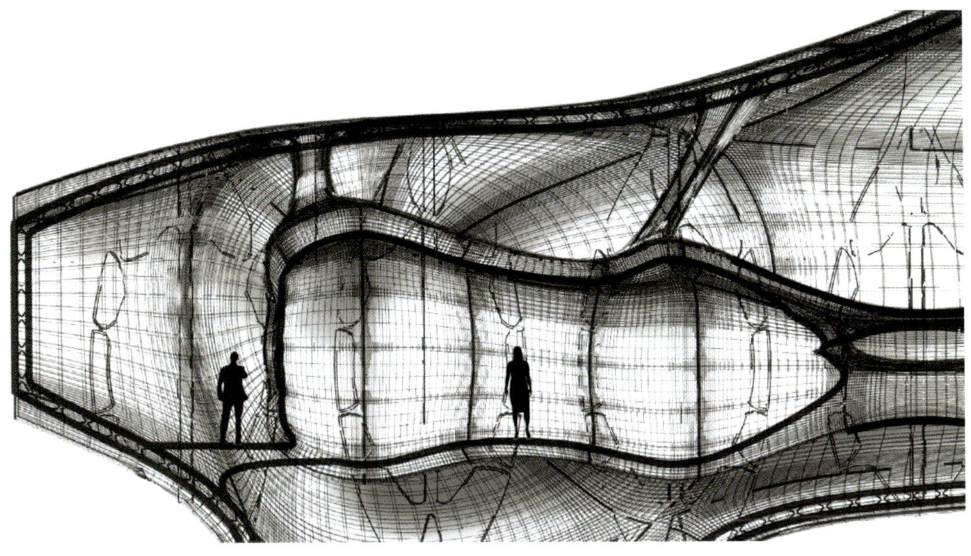

Top: Interior views of proto-architectural morpholoy showing spatial quality, apertures, and functional seams.

Bottom: Section of proto-architectural morphology.

2014 Final Studio Review featuring guest critics: Brandon Clifford, Marc Fornes, Axel Kilian, Neil Leach, Panagiotis Michalatos, Jenny Sabin.

# Critics' Responses

2013 Final Studio Review featuring guest critics: Martin Bechthold, Johan Bettum, and Panagiotis Michalatos.

## Mid Review Critics

**2013** Sean Ahlquist, Mark Fornes, Mariana Ibañez, Aleks Jaeschke, Axel Kilian, Panagiotis Michalatos, Etien Santiago

**2014** Leire Asensio-Villoria, Brandon Clifford, Marc Goulthorpe, Aleksandra Jaeschke, Axel Kilian, Panagiotis Michalatos

**2015** Leire Asensio-Villoria, Axel Kilian, Panagiotis Michalatos

## Final Review Critics

**2013** Martin Bechthold, Johan Bettum, Marc Fornes, Mariana Ibañez, Hauke Jungjohann, Sanford Kwinter, Panagiotis Michalatos

**2014** Brandon Clifford, Marc Fornes, Axel Kilian, Neil Leach, Panagiotis Michalatos, Jenny Sabin

**2015** Brandon Clifford, Mariana Ibañez, Axel Kilian, Panagiotis Michalatos, Jenny Sabin

# What is the Question?

Johan Bettum

The difficult relation between fibrous composite systems and architecture can be illustrated by the metaphor of the Butterfly Effect which, derived from chaos theory, suggests that small causes in one realm may have enormous effects in another. That is to say, how do the material geometry and geometrical inter-relations of fibers on scales down to $10^{-3}$ produce effects on the scale of buildings? For three-quarters of a century architects have anticipated these effects, even described them as revolutionary. Yet, as far as buildings and construction go, there is little to deny that the visionary qualities of the first generation of fibrous-composite projects (early 1950s to 1973) have eclipsed most subsequent work with these material systems.

There are at least two major reasons why working with fibrous-composite systems is so difficult. One is that these systems are not materials in the classical sense but designed concoctions of various material sub-systems. This means that fibrous-composite systems evade existing material epistemology and categorization as well as much of our expertise and assessment standards. The typical version for architectural use consists of one or another fibrous composition as reinforcement embedded in a polymer matrix that guarantees cohesion and surface continuity. The fibrous reinforcement is also a material system and thus given by inter-relations between parts where the fibrous unit is defined by its aspect ratio, that is, the geometrically given ratio between the cross section and length of the fiber. Since these material and geometrical variables are given on minuscule scales and co-dependent on neighbouring variables, the architectural design task becomes vast, staggeringly multifaceted, and complex.

The other major reason why the use of these material systems date have not engendered a unique expression and possible new forms of architecture is that the vastness of the problem has led to false assumptions about what is at stake and excruciating simplifications of the problem at hand. For instance, the minute and difficult inter-relational dynamics of fibrous geometry has become replaced by a quasi-textile appearance of material composition on a building



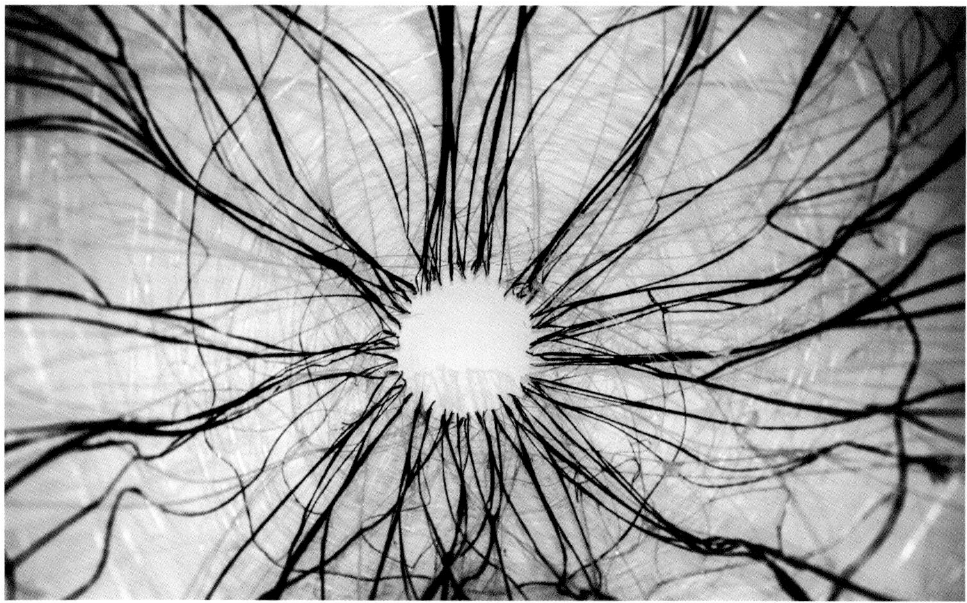

2015 Research Project *Soft Design: Behavioral Form Finding* by Marysol Rivas Brito, Gavin Ruedisueli.

scale. Likewise, the simple but delicate composite relation between reinforcement and matrix has recently been replaced by an obsession with fibers and textiles only. Moreover, the typical invocation of Gottfried Semper's work on textiles—Semper's genius and many insights notwithstanding—has little bearing on contemporary fibrous composites in architecture. No wonder, then, that visions for how these material systems may present architecture with new opportunities too often end up in substitutional practices: Stylistic imitation of Greek columns and pediments in malls, discrete panelization where other materials work perfectly well (Zaha Hadid for Chanel) and endless fiber projects whose newness principally echoes known rebar plans in a contrived pursuit of one or another form of material optimization. Much of this harks back to the question of scale, yet the overriding question is: What is the design problem?

In this context new technology presents the significant change, since the material systems were introduced for building construction along with postwar industrialization of the Western world. For instance, until recently and for technological as well as economical reasons, the standard fibrous reinforcement in composite systems used staple fibers that are cut into discrete lengths instead of continuous fibers. Increased digital computational capacities represent the most important change as it enables access to ever-smaller material and system scales for design and fabrication purposes. The best work of Achim Menges and colleagues, including that in Menges's design studios on Fibrous Tectonics at GSD, comprises the most advanced and groundbreaking efforts to break away from the historical tendency to see technological improvements change tools and methods but lead to "little more than transferring traditional [...] procedures to the operation of machinery."[1] Specifically, when Purisic, Varholick, Gao, and Safaverdi in the 2015 GSD studio experiment with traditional knitting techniques in a dynamical relation with pneumatic membranes, they succeed in tapping into the power of textile mechanics and geometry to produce startlingly beautiful and fresh architectural effects. The achievement depends by and large on their detailed engagement with the fibers/yarns and their inter-looping and includes the formation of apertures in the surfaces, pinching and pleating that engenders embedded, local forms and a highly variegated surface topology.

However, their most impressive achievement is to benefit from the knitted form's elasticity to design the rich architectural geometry while exploiting the inherent spatiality embedded in textiles and not compromising on the needed material saturation. It is the latter material saturation that is the endemic forfeiture when the scalar refinement of fibers and textiles is ignored.

1 C. D. Elliot, *Technics and Architecture: The Development of Materials and Systems for Building*, (Cambridge: The MIT Press, 1992), 2.

2015 Research Project *An Architectonic Notion For Knitting And Pneumatics* by Yuan Gao, Demir Purisic, Zahra Safaverdi, Joseph Varholick.

# Fibrous Structures Studio

Axel Kilian

As an invited critic to the three-year fibrous structures studio led by Achim Menges at the Harvard GSD, I had the opportunity to experience firsthand and comment on the studio's work and development. As an accumulative research studio fibrous structures stands out among architectural design studios for maintaining a very focused and consistent research agenda over a three-year period. The studios progressively explored more in-depth experiments on fibrous structures using mostly carbon and fiberglass strand composites.

The studio explorations started with fixed winding rigs to overcome the dependency on large-scale one-time use molds, traditionally used in composite lay-up structures. These rigs were developed geometrically, then laser cut. Parallel algorithms were developed for the winding sequence to achieve the desired surface results. In the early experiments, the physical behavior of the fibers played an important role as secondary layers would come to rest on the hyperbolic surface defined by the first set of strands. Based on friction and tension the equilibrium would slip into geodesic paths on these surfaces. This combination of geometric and material computation creates a number of very intriguing surface explorations, culminating in some of the most refined projects in the second year of the studio series.

An important extension to the surface-based fibrous organization was started in the 2014 studio with *Pneumatic Fibrous Form* by Erin Cuevas, Mike Johnson, and Jana Masset. This project explores fiber organization in a volumetric fashion, cross-connecting fibers between multi-layered fiber surfaces. This theme was substantially expanded on by Yuan Gao, Demir Purisic, Zahra Safaverdi, and Joe Varholick in *An Architectonic Notion for Knitting and Pneumatics* through their investigations using pneumatic molds in combination with parametrically controlled knitting to control the surface membranes.

The design development throughout the groups happened in parallel with very refined prototype developments, calibrating the concept with the material computation of the constructs. All of the individual groups went to great depth to document and communicate their research process and procedural fabrication processes through notational diagram, thereby sharing their approach for possible future exploration. This sharing of detailed knowledge is a key requirement for a multi-year research effort allowing follow-up groups to build on the preceding work. In addition, the studio series benefited from the parallel research developed at ICD at the University of Stuttgart that was shared in parts through visiting researchers from Stuttgart. These researchers ran workshops as part of the studio series in Cambridge. This is a promising model for the research-studio concept as a bridge between research and teaching, allowing both researchers and students to benefit from each other's contributions.

The clear focus on fibrous structures produced a breadth of approaches that were explored in depth. This research went beyond work merely inspired by biomimetic principles, or the often incomplete prototypical exploration in more holistic studios (where development is often shortened due to project requirements). This is not to be misunderstood as a proposal in which research would generally stand over architectural design development, but as an argument in support of the research studio model as an essential component in the overall approach to teaching design studios. The biggest challenge that remains is to develop the fibrous structures research findings beyond the proto architectures of the design explorations shown here. Can the rich material and spatial qualities that were developed carry over to influence architecture? Or do they simply substitute established material regimes? I think it is clear that the various student projects have shown a deep integration of material culture with novel scale-specific fabrication processes. These projects push fibrous structures knowledge beyond the established fiber-composite industrial usage and practices into the domain of architecture. However, much work remains to develop an architectural design response based on these fascinating and provoking reports.

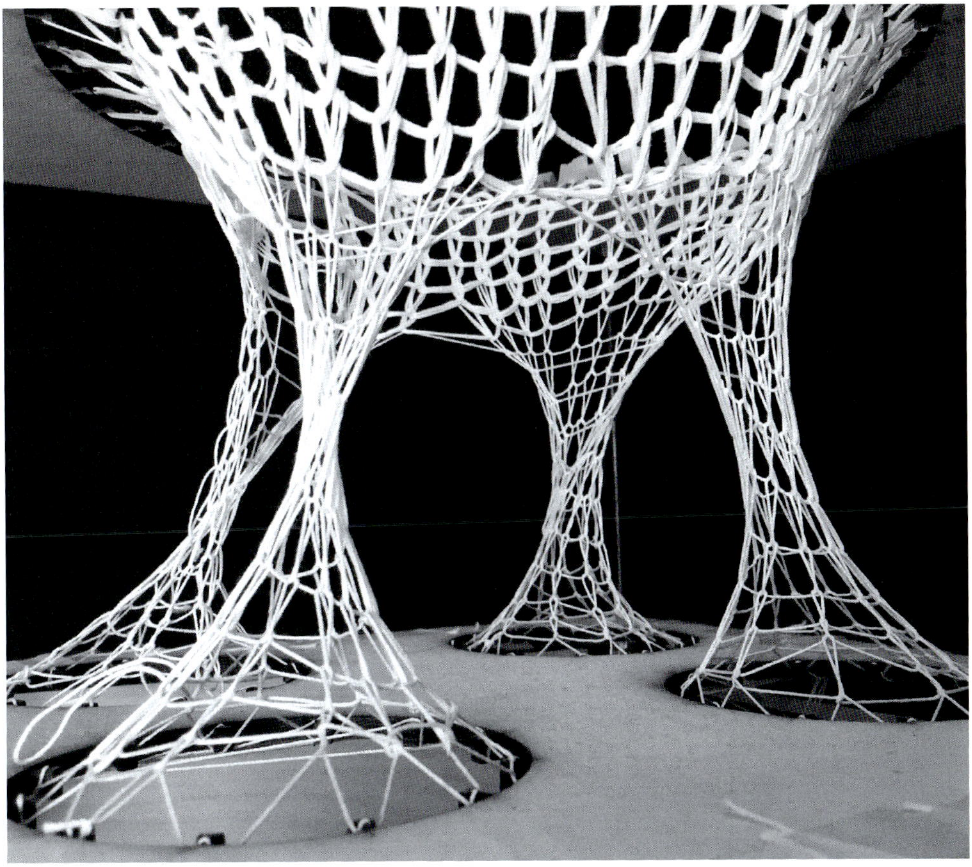

Top: 2015 Research Project *An Architectonic Notion for Knitting and Pneumatics* by Yuan Gao, Demir Purisic, Zahra Safaverdi, Joseph Varholick.

Bottom: 2014 Research Project *Pneumatic Fibrous Form* by Erin Cuevas, Mike Johnson, Jana Masset.

# Biosynthetic Digital Handcraft

**Jenny Sabin**

> *Frei Otto also took up the notion of self-generation and the analogy between biology and building, but eschewed the imitation of nature in favor of working directly in materials to produce models that were at once natural and artificial.*
>
> *At the same time, he also eschewed their translation into a universalizing mathesis. Rather than focusing on form or formula, he took the idea of analogy in an entirely different direction, preferring to stage experiments in which materials find their own form.*
>
> —From Detlef Mertins, *Bioconstructivisms*

Upon first participating on Menges's final review in December 2014 at the Harvard GSD, I walked into the pit mesmerized by the material beauty and intricacy of the fibrous models, each one telling a rigorous tale of process, materially directed generative design, and digital handcraft. Laser-cut jigs filtering and organizing hundreds of well-placed strands; balloons arrayed in a matrix generating pneumatic assemblages akin to cells enmeshed in their extracellular matrix; shells and composites impregnated with resin and regions of carbon-fiber; ribs organizing strands in continuous closed-curve networks; human-sized composite surfaces and panels; fibril networks and fibrous assemblages generating thick components and larger architectural elements. These were but a few of the models that I examined. I looked closer as the review commenced, pausing to decipher between what had been made by hand versus what had been digitally fabricated. This was, after all, a Menges review. I struggled to understand the process, and finally asked, "So, you placed each carbon strand by hand?" Where were the dancing industrial robots delicately winding carbon-fiber based on natural systems producing highly differentiated morphologies for novel composite shell structures? Having visited Menges's ICD at Stuttgart the previous summer, I saw first-hand the robotic fabrication process that they had innovated involving two interacting 6-axis robots to produce doubly curved glass- and carbon-fiber reinforced polymers through a winding process. Through this simple process, which basically entails winding layers of fibers and strategically impregnating the hollow cores with resin, 36 unique components were generated for a lightweight pavilion. Perhaps due to a lack of resources and space, and partially due to time restrictions, robotic fabrication was largely absent from the Fibrous Tectonic studio at the Harvard GSD. I was positively surprised to see the strong presence of digital handcraft and analog modeling in conjunction with sophisticated digital simulations, a process saturated in material and computation, but largely analogic.



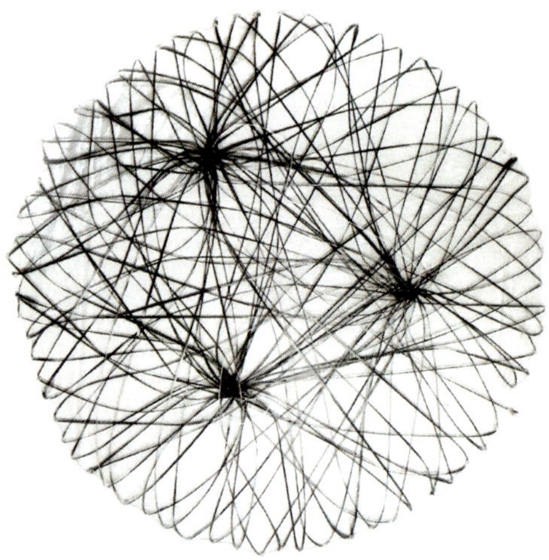

2015 Research Project *Soft Control Fiber System* by Feijiao Huo, Xin Ji, Man Su, Junko Yamamoto.

I returned the second year for the final review held in December 2015, where again the studio focused on fibrous tectonics and materially driven generative design, but with a stronger emphasis upon bioinspired models. In one project, the four principles of fibrous structures found in the natural world were discussed: hierarchy, heterogeneity, anisotropy, and redundancy. The models were more voluminous, making use of textile processes such as knitting to explore these biological principles through material analogs. Here, holes and ladders generate knots and openings in the knit system, a continuous deposition of material, one link and row to the next. Volumes were grafted to the next, synthetically exploring hierarchy and more mature architectural morphologies. Failures and messy computation become opportunities as the assemblages adapt and design intuition is honed through the agency of the material and process. Perhaps the most important aspect of the studio concerns the development of a design process saturated in material computation and making as steered and specified by a biological model or dynamic template. Here, the intention is not merely about mimicking biology, but learning how to design like nature, opportunistically extracting principles and processes for novel tectonic systems. The studio operates across scales through the explicit exploration of biological models for novel structures in the context of computational matter. While nonlinear concepts are widely applied in analysis and generative design, they have not yet convincingly translated into the material realm of fabrication and construction in architecture. The work in this studio offers some clues and answers where possible design routes and techniques no longer privilege column, beam, and arch through a broadened definition of architectural tectonics successfully made with advancements in computational design. How might these advancements impact material practice in architecture, engineering, and construction at economic, technological and cultural levels?

While these questions remain unanswered, one of the most important deliverables of the studio concerns fostering new habits of thought and material intuition where nonstandard tectonic elements emerge through the rigorous investigation of the behaviors of natural models and their corresponding translation into novel material systems. Here, geometry, materiality, pattern, structure, and form are inextricably linked. Menges and his students resist the post-rationalization of complex form through an approach that engages materially directed generative design. Here, architectural affordances reveal themselves as evolving flows of force through geometry and matter that are computed, designed, and fabricated through analog robotic interfaces that dance, collaborate, wind, and weave. These transformative models may in parallel provide potent contributions toward issues of construction, digital fabrication, and material ecologies in architecture. Critical to this approach are design processes rooted in experimentation without predetermination of form. Here, emphasis is placed upon the dynamics of natural models, of behavior and process in the material formation of difference and heterogeneous entities.

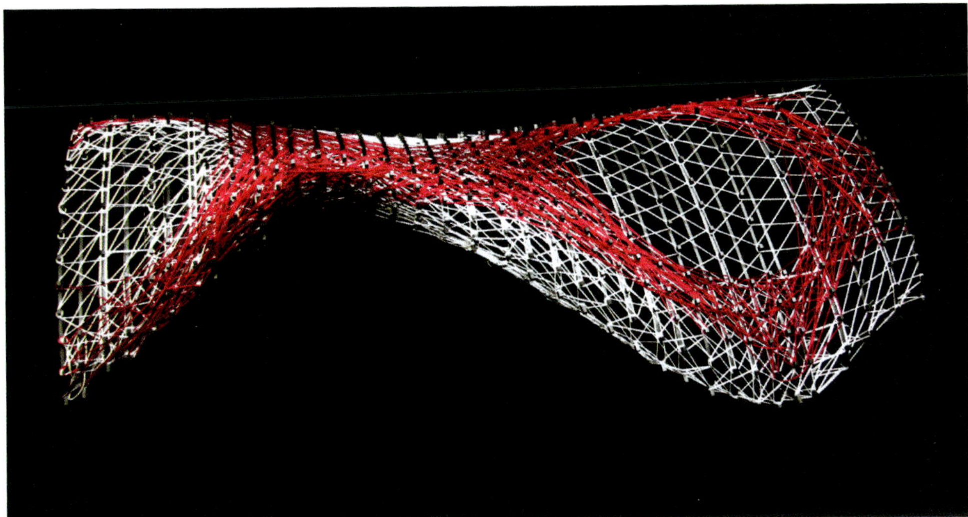

2013 Research Project *Skin as Structure: A Fibrous Architectural Protoype* by Catherine Soderberg.

2013 Final Studio Review featuring guest critics: Panagiotis Michalatos, Johan Bettum, Martin Bechthold, Mariana Ibañez.

### Achim Menges

Achim Menges is a registered architect and Professor at Stuttgart University where he is the Founding Director of the Institute for Computational Design. Since 2009, he has been a Visiting Professor in Architecture at the Harvard University Graduate School of Design. He graduated with honors from the AA School of Architecture.

### Moritz Dörstelmann

Moritz Dörstelmann is a Research Associate and Doctoral Candidate at the Institute for Computational Design at Stuttgart University. He studied architecture at the RWTH Aachen University and the University of Applied Arts in Vienna where he graduated with distinction from the master class of Zaha Hadid and Patrik Schumacher.

### Marshall Prado

Marshall Prado is a Research Associate at the Institute for Computational Design at Stuttgart University. He holds a Bachelor of Architecture from North Carolina State University and advanced degrees as a Master of Architecture and a Master of Design Studies in Technology from the Harvard University Graduate School of Design.

### Johan Bettum

Johan Bettum is a Professor of Architecture and Program Director of the Städelschule Architecture Class. He studied at the AA School of Architecture after receiving a BA in biology from Princeton University, and holds a PhD in Design from Oslo School of Architecture and Design.

Axel Kilian

Axel Kilian is an Assistant Professor in Computational Design at Princeton University. He received a degree in Architecture from University of the Arts Berlin, and holds advanced degrees as a Master of Science in Architecture Studies (SMarchS) and PhD in Design and Computation from Massachusetts Institute of Technology.

Jenny Sabin

Jenny Sabin is an Assistant Professor in Architecture and Director of Graduate Studies at Cornell University's AAP. She runs Jenny Sabin Studio and Sabin Design Lab. She completed a Master of Architecture with honors from the University of Pennsylvania, and holds bachelor degrees in Visual Art and Ceramics from University of Washington.

## Colophon

Material Performance:
Fibrous Tectonics &
Architectural Morphology

**Instructors**
Achim Menges
**Report Design**
A. Scottie McDaniel

A Harvard University Graduate
School of Design Publication

**Dean and Alexander and Victoria Wiley Professor of Design**
Mohsen Mostafavi
**Editor in Chief**
Jennifer Sigler
**Publications Coordinator**
Meghan Sandberg
**Editorial Support**
Claire Barliant, Travis Dagenais

Series design by Laura Grey and Zak Jensen

ISBN 978-1-934510-57-5



Acknowledgments

I would like to express my sincere gratitude to the Harvard GSD for their interest in making this venture possible and for their generous support of the studio. I am equally thankful to the students for their fantastic effort, tremendous talent, and sheer dedication to explore the design research field presented in this publication. I would also like to thank my colleagues at the ICD for their expert advice and workshops, and the ICD/ITKE at the University of Stuttgart for the development of some of the decisive enabling technologies and for the inspiration of the Research Pavilions. Lastly, I'd like to acknowledge the Getty Lab for supporting the Harvard GSD and ICD research, and for their contribution to this publication.

Image Credits

Student groups were responsible for all documentation of their projects. All final review photos were taken by photographer Justin Knight.

Cover: 2014 Research Project *Nature of Bi-stability in Composite Structures* by Niccolo Dambrosio, Ping Lu, Stefan Stanojevic.

The editors have attempted to acknowledge all sources of images used and apologize for any errors or omissions.

Harvard University
Graduate School of Design
48 Quincy Street
Cambridge, MA 02138

publications@gsd.harvard.edu
gsd.harvard.edu